GHOST TOWNS OF NEW ENGLAND

Twenty-Six Locations Lost to Time

TARYN PLUMB

Down East Books

Camden, Maine

Down East Books

An imprint of Globe Pequot, a trade division of
The Rowman & Littlefield Publishing Group, Inc.
4501 Forbes Blvd., Ste. 200
Lanham, MD 20706
www.rowman.com

Distributed by NATIONAL BOOK NETWORK

British Library Cataloguing in Publication Information available

Library of Congress Cataloging-in-Publication Data available

ISBN 978-1-68475-016-0 (paperback)
ISBN 978-1-68475-017-7 (e-book)

♾™ The paper used in this publication meets the minimum requirements of American National
Standard for Information Sciences—Permanence of Paper for Printed Library Materials, ANSI/
NISO Z39.48-1992.

We have all experienced abandon—and to be abandoned
is to truly gain an understanding of oneself.

Contents

CONTENTS

INTRODUCTION

And you will face the sea of darkness, and all therein that may be explored.

—LUCIO FULCI

Kenopsia

n. The eerie, forlorn atmosphere of a place that is usually bustling with people but is now abandoned and quiet . . . an emotional afterimage that makes it seem not just empty but hyper-empty, with a total population in the negative.

Ghost towns. The mind immediately conjures the old west archetype: rough-hewn assemblages of stores, saloons, boarding houses, and brothels standing in contrast to the desert.

But here, too, in New England, there have been numerous towns abandoned, neglected, wiped, or washed out or made obsolete.

Former mill, mining, and logging communities representing humankind's propensity to descend in waves on valuable resources, then just as hastily depart when those have been depleted. Onetime villages mercilessly drowned in the name of progress. Erstwhile beachside hamlets and lavish resorts eternally shunned by tourists. Towns whose inhabitants simply vanished—sometimes, truly overnight—or were cruelly expelled; others whose populations achingly withered.

They were discarded with the precipitous rises and falls of industry, economy, culture—or in some cases, due to sheer survival necessity.

Their remains left falling into ruin are often cloaked in the midst of the overgrown lands where they were once prominent—mere fragments, hints, shadows. In some cases, they have left behind tangible remnants: cellar holes, stone walls, and other structures sinking back into the earth they once claimed and lost among trees that have defiantly grown up amidst them; once well-maintained paths and roads leading off to some oblivion; tombstones blanched and scoured by time slanted against one another as if in comfort.

Some have been saved; others reclaimed or repurposed; many, in more recent years, attracting the morbidly curious, the historically inclined, the seekers of the paranormal. They have become asterisks to history or comprise more substantial paragraphs and chapters in humankind's playbook. They are contrastingly richly detailed, or scantily, sterilely documented.

Because the region was the first in the country to be settled by colonists, the number of ghost towns is immeasurable; certainly, too many to include here.

They are but whispers, sighs, of what they once were. And if we listen closely, we can hear their stories.

Part I

Maine

The largest land-wise of the New England states, Maine is abundant with natural resources—hundreds of miles of coastline; thousands of offshore islands; rivers, lakes, ponds, mountains, forests, fields, even a desert.

All that space has also meant that many a town has come and gone—built up, torn down, washed away, rebuilt, or left to disappear back into the earth.

ONE

BOOBYTOWN

Expelling the Poor, Tired, Weary

THEY LIVED IN EARTHEN MOUNDS, DUGOUTS IN THE SIDES OF hills, underground caves, or ramshackle, crudely assembled log cabins—families crammed together into close, primitive quarters, often right alongside their livestock. Some resorted to wearing shingles for shoes or subsisted on what berries and raw dandelions they could scavenge.

They were the outcasts, the unmentionables, the Misérables, left to fend for themselves in the rough Maine wilderness.

Cities are often ashamed of their poor and destitute. There's the old cliché—based, unfortunately, on real-life circumstances—of those living on the "wrong side of the tracks," the projects, the areas of town that "good people" go out of their way to avoid.

Somewhere around the quarter-century or half-century mark of the 1800s, Lewiston, Maine, decided to do something about its deplorable "unwashed." The once prospering mill city was experiencing an economic depression, and its growing population of the poverty-stricken, beggars, and so-called freeloaders were straining its welfare budget—and, as far as city leaders, businessmen, and the more fortunate Lewistonians were considered, something had to be done.

The solution? Round up these unwanted and unwelcome and ship them out of Lewiston some 85 miles away to the Lower Dallas/Rangeley area all the way up in the mountainous northwest corner of the state (not far from Maine's ragged, present-day border with Quebec).

As noted in a February 1877 issue of Lewiston's *Evening Journal*: "These undesirables were moved at a distance of untold miles into the wilderness of northern Maine."

A MEAGER EXISTENCE

Not long after relocation, the area came to be known as "Boobytown"—named for its most populous French-Canadian immigrant Bubier family. At one time, there were estimated to be 200 people living in the settlement's squalor.

The outcasts were given some potato seeds, occasional provisions, and annual trifling relief funds by their former city, but were otherwise left to build their own makeshift housing and survive in what more recent vernacular would be considered shantytowns or "tent cities."

One of the Bubiers, for example, was cramped into a two-room shack with his wife and six children; half of this space, however, was reserved for the family cow. The *Evening Journal* reported that they had no chairs or beds, and that the paterfamilias and his brood were dressed in sewn-together rags, were unable to read or write, and that they resorted to sleeping on the cold dirt floor.

Many more residents lived in filthy conditions alongside pigs and chickens. Reports were that there was no doctor in town, and that none ever visited the impoverished colony.

Still, Boobytowners somehow managed to survive by gathering berries and other greens; growing a paltry number of potatoes, cabbages, and wheat; and hunting and fishing. Much of this was hauled for miles to nearby towns to trade for more substantial provisions.

Despite their living conditions and way of life, they were considered by more affluent locals to be honest, fair-trading, and hard-working (for what little they had to work with, that is). And in fact, more Bubiers than any other family in the Rangeley area served in the Civil War.

For its part, Lewiston's support of the downtrodden colony ranged from $100 to $500 a year depending on available funding and the general public's feelings of generosity. An 1856 annual report of the overseer of the poor, for example, claimed doling out "on account of persons off the poor farm"—namely the Bubiers—$176.14. Nine years later, in 1865, residents were collectively given $168.79.

Conditions improved, ever so slightly, when the narrow-gauge railroad came into adjacent Rangeley; the Sandy River and Rangeley Lakes Railroad was the longest of five two-foot-wide railways that once serviced the state and were unique to Maine.

Boobytowners began to eke out livings by lumbering and manufacturing shingles that were transported via train to more populated environs. And the shingles served a double purpose: One Paul Bunyan-sized Bubier was said to wear them as shoes, even heating them up in the winter to stand on while chopping wood or performing other chores (this because his family owned only one pair of shoes and used them sparingly). That same Bubier purportedly became so hungry at times that he ate dandelions, raw and directly from the field like a grazing animal.

With the advent of the railroad, residents also erected a saw-mill and schoolhouse, where regular Sunday services were held by amateur town preachers. Ministers from adjacent towns did pass through the settlement once in a great while, and they and other visitors—what few there were—were shocked at the deplorable conditions. One local genealogical researcher, Shirley Adams, wrote about two Lewiston overseers who visited the colony in 1875 and returned with a "very melancholy report."

Despite some resultant public outcry from Lewistonians, Boo-bytowners refused to be relocated back to Lewiston. Because it was all they knew—and perhaps they were still irked at being thrown out of the city—many continued with their scant existences in the Franklin County wilderness.

Eventually, though, the Sandy River Rangeley Lakes Railroad ceased to run. (Today, a nonprofit is dedicated to preserving and restoring it.) The mills soon shut down and Boobytowners began to filter away.

The area became abandoned. Many of the Bubiers, perhaps to shed their family's label of poverty, replaced their surnames with Flagg, Thomas, and Withey (or Whitney). Many of them are buried in the Bubier Cemetery in Upper Dallas or the Bubier-Green-Stuart Cemetery in Dallas Plantation. Their dozen or so headstones range from the 1840s to the 1940s, but many more remain unmarked.

Much like the eschewed names, not much exists in public record of Boobytown: Many documents pertaining to its existence were destroyed when the Lewiston City Hall burned beyond rec-ognition in 1890.

Popular opinion seems to dictate that the village of outcasts remains a black mark on Maine history—one that many, including its now deceased residents and their ancestors, would rather wipe from memory.

Two

DAVIDSON

The Community Away

THE TOWN WAS ONCE TEEMING WITH LIFE: NUMEROUS HOMES and families; a hall with lively dances and screenings of "moving pictures"; teams of dozens of horses that hauled lumber from the outlying woods; a thrumming factory; prize, award-winning Holstein cows that people from all over came to view and purchase during "Field Days."

But the small community of Davidson in north-central Maine had a short, albeit thriving, lifespan. After just a couple of decades, the unorganized township simply ceased to be—a casualty of the 1929 stock market crash, the ensuing Depression, and a floundering lumber trade.

Today, not much is known about life there, besides the semi-fictionalized account, "Ollie's Davidson" by Nina Way Lord. Penned in 1988 and based on her family's experiences, the book shows us the lumbering and factory town in 1922 through the eyes of a ten-year-old girl.

Way Lord laments of the loss: "It is time that someone wrote a story about Davidson, lest even the memory of it depart."

Located west of Stacyville, nestled at the base of Mt. Katahdin and present-day Baxter State Park, the land that would come to be Davidson was purchased by Ora Gilpatrick in 1901.

At the time, the six-and-a-half-mile tract containing roughly 25,000 acres was so thick with timber that "one would hardly have noticed, from the train, the little lake, known as Davidson Pond, upon the shore of which the little hamlet of Davidson now nestles," notes a writeup from the late 1910s.

Still, the wealthy Gilpatricks never had any intentions of establishing a town.

Ora, a bank president and successful businessman versed in the lumbering trade, simply had the goal to cut the profitable timber on the unsettled, heavily wooded land and then move on—thinking that this could be accomplished in about ten years.

But as later reported, "Ten years, a dozen years, rolled by with the end still a long way off."

Gilpatrick and his sons Victor and Rex then decided to clear a small portion of their holdings to operate a dairy farm to supplement their successful Summit Lumber Co. With a keen eye on further expansion, they soon came up with the idea to manufacture clothespins from the timber they harvested. A mill went up, as did several homes, two boarding houses and a one-room schoolhouse; a town office, post office, general store, blacksmith shop and dairy; not to mention a combined dancing hall and cinema. The town was even furnished with wooden sidewalks, which became a source of pride for residents.

The nearby railway also laid tracks into town, and the town once boasted a station where trains stopped six times daily (except on Sundays).

At its height, Davidson had 92 horse teams that hauled lumber from the outlying woods, and its mill employed 65 women and men who churned out 123.8 million pins a year. It was said that the wooden block used to make them, if laid end to end, would have extended 9,722 miles—or roughly two-fifths of the distance around the world.

Davidson Summit Farm, meanwhile, shipped daily loads of milk and cream; it also produced one hundred acres—or about ten railcar loads—of potatoes and 5,000 bushels of oats every year.

Then there were its prized Holsteins. The first was purchased in 1913, and ensuing offspring were known for their excellence, garnering state, and New England champion records. In fact, the town held "Field Days" that attracted people from all around. An early clipping from the *Bangor Daily News* even described the farm and its expositions as one of Maine's best.

Several generations of cattle were bred and sold, with sales literature at the time listing their ages, butter and milk outputs, and (at least to those not familiar with the trade) droll names and descriptions.

For example, one six-year-old "dam" (or the mother of a calf) produced 876 pounds of butter and 23,000 gallons of milk in a year (making her a record-holder). Another four-year-old dam produced 30.50 pounds of butter and 659.1 gallons of milk over a seven-day period.

These female and male cows and bulls bore names like King Walker Johanna, Summit Sarcastic Beets, Roxland Brua Korndyke, and Summit Lota Huntress. Ads noted of one of the original foundation cows, Blanche Pauline de Kol: "You should be interested in her daughter and granddaughter and other relatives," while Marion Walker de Kol the second was plainly described as thus: "Maybe you would rather have her son." And Marion Clover Blossom the third? She was "a New England champion developed in the herd." But "she is now old and blemished."

One brochure from the 1910s emphasized: "REMEMBER: The Summit Lumber Co. has never gone in for extreme production. The herd was founded for practical reasons and has been operated upon a practical basis." The policy has been a normal production with the cows producing calves regularly, and cattle have not been "stuffed to the limit with the highly concentrated feeds . . . the result has been good strong rigorous calves and a healthy profitable herd at the pail."

A WAY OF LIFE

In her memoir, Way Lord underscores townspeople's admiration of their resident Holsteins, as well as their delight in Davidson's celebrated field days.

She also describes the wealthy Gilpatricks, who owned the largest houses in town and had their own private wells, and other notable family names such as Estabrook, Nye, Boone, Knox, Moody, Smith, and Cameron. Twenty-five to thirty women spent their days "packin' clothes pins" on both hot and cold days in the "weather-beaten" factory sprawled beside Davidson Lake (which was unsuitable for swimming or fishing on account of its sinking, muddy bottom). Male and female coworkers lived in separate boarding houses, while lumbermen lived in camps in the woods all year round.

For his part, her father worked in the dark, low-ceilinged blacksmith shop, while her mother washed men's shirts for ten cents apiece. And since Davidson was an unorganized township, the state looked after its school, with the state superintendent coming in a few times a year from the Augusta capital.

There was a woman from Sherman who visited once a week to give music lessons for a quarter a piece; a peddler from Millinocket who hawked her wares twice a month; various tramps who hopped off railcars only to be rounded up by residents.

Way Lord also fondly recalls children roaming through the surrounding thick woods but never getting lost, and the movies and dances that were held each week in the gathering hall. The silent picture showings cost a dime, while dances were free (and quite a sight, as the normally quiet, drably attired girls who worked in the mill dressed up in their finest and drew stares from all that passed).

Ultimately, she writes, "Ollie couldn't imagine why anyone would want to leave Davidson."

But in the end, they had no choice. The year 1929 brought along with it the decimating Black Friday, prompting the Gilpatricks to sell Davidson to a Maine senator. Lumbering operations slowed, then halted, the mill shut down, and by 1931 what was once a town was no longer. The hard-working Yankees who lived, worked, and raised their families there began filtering out to other places.

Today, intrepid explorers to the remote, overgrown site can find scant remnants of foundations; one large collapsing brick smoke-stack, another of metal felled and disintegrating; a moss-covered safe and other indiscernible metal fragments. With time, they continue to crumble and rust as they are absorbed by the earth.

"Only trees, wild animals, and memories remain," Way Lord laments of the town, lost even to time 35 years ago at the time of her writing. "This is not even a ghost town, for there's no longer a place for a ghost to hang out, unless he could cling to part of a crumbling wall, hidden in overgrown bushes."

And she offers the simple but somber eulogy: "The town is no more."

THREE

FLAGSTAFF

Drowned in the Name of Progress

ALL OF A SUDDEN, IT REAPPEARED LIKE A WATERY PHOENIX.

In winter 1979, drought caused Flagstaff Lake—which had been raised in 1949 to create a reservoir and support a large system of dams downstream along the Kennebec River—to recede, and the Dead River flowed through the area once more.

So, thirty years after it was sacrificed, as if to commemorate a somber anniversary, the remnants of the small town of Flagstaff rose (briefly) from the depths of the lake that had drowned it.

Locals marveled at the ability to walk the hamlet's Main Street once again, and to find that, despite being submerged in water for decades, its tar roads were still mostly intact, even solid. Even though much of the town had been dismantled and burned to make way for the reservoir, many cellar holes remained; some old timers could ably locate the stone foundations of their former homes and those of their neighbors and friends.

Also visible were the rotting remains of machinery that once provided electricity for much of the town; gas pumps at one of the local general stores; fragments of a hotel and boat rental that had once been a popular destination for locals and out-of-towners alike.

And the long cement steps of another town store rose up to the sky as if in defiance of its demise.

As the drought abated and the former town was once again swallowed up by water, the brief glimpse of its ruins was a stark reminder of all that had been literally washed away in mankind's constant quest for progress.

Between 1949 and 1950, the small Maine towns of Flagstaff and Dead River were flooded beneath Flagstaff Lake and residents were forced to relocate or raze their homes and evacuate. With little notice and no choice, many complied; yet some holdouts didn't.

Today Flagstaff Lake is the fourth largest in Maine (a state known for its thousands of water bodies, big and small), that supports the Long Falls Dam, which regulates the flow of Dead River into the Kennebec. With a surface area of 20,300 acres, its storage capacity is more than 275,000 acre-feet.

Flooding of towns for reservoirs and dams is a practice that goes back decades—an unfortunate price to support national growth. For the benefit of the majority, many have had to make great sacrifices.

Which was the ultimate fate of Flagstaff and Dead River, a forfeiture that continues to resonate to this day.

BEFORE THE FLOOD

With a combined population of a mere few hundred residents, the two towns were located in the northwestern Maine mountains just twenty-some odd miles from the Quebec border. The Dead River snaked through their low-lying location, and their townships offered handsome views of Bigelow Mountain.

And while the origins of the name Dead River seem to be lost to time, the roots for Flagstaff—both the town and the name— hold a unique place in history.

In the early days of the American Revolutionary War in the fall of 1775, Benedict Arnold and a detachment of 1,100 men were on their way to attack the British stronghold in Quebec. Following the Kennebec River, they first paused at Fort Western (in the modern-day capital of Augusta), then again battened down for respite at the base of a long mountain ridge. So, the story goes, a flagstaff (or flagpole) was erected from a tall juniper tree, and Major Timothy Bigelow climbed to the summit "for the purpose of observation."

The contingent moved on, the flagstaff was left behind, and the mountain was eventually named after the major who hardily ascended it. And until the town was engulfed in water in 1950, a flagstaff continuously marked that very spot.

Settlers began arriving in the early part of the nineteenth century, lured by the timber resources and the rich soil in the Dead River floodplain. They cleared the land for cabins, a sawmill and gristmill, then family homes, a church, school, post office, general store, blacksmith shop, community hall, and even a small hotel.

By 1860, Flagstaff was a thriving plantation, and it was described in a volume of *History and Description of New England* as having some "excellent farming land," while its families were making "good progress in the settlement." Those families included Viles, Savages, Wings, Hines, and Taylors, and their heads of households made livings as lumbermen, rivermen, and guides. At the time of the Civil War, Flagstaff's population was around 75; Dead River's was roughly 100.

For the next near-century, the towns remained vibrant—despite their remote locations—continuing to grow and establish themselves in the lumbering and recreation trades.

That was, until 1949.

THE FLOODWATERS

The first tolls of the death knell actually started several decades earlier, with Walter Scott Wyman, co-founder of Central Maine Power (CMP), who is credited with the widespread electrification of the state. A native of Oakland, Maine, who studied electrical engineering at Tufts University, he and business partner Harvey Eaton began their enterprise with a simple generator; this provided street lighting and electric service to about 100 residents of his hometown.

But the pair quickly expanded their sights and reach, purchasing small electrical producers across central and northern Maine to create the overreaching CMP entity (founded in 1910, still in existence today and servicing much of the state). They began building hydroelectric dams, combining the electrical output of absorbed companies and also purchased controlling shares in Maine's largest cotton textile mills and began renovating their obsolete, decades-old power systems.

Because continued population growth and burgeoning industry required more output, Wyman and Eaton identified the need for a large-scale dam and reservoir that could control the waters of the Kennebec River.

For this purpose, it didn't take them long to focus in on Flagstaff Pond—the location was prime because it was the only one of any size with an elevation low enough to be covered by a future reservoir. Such an endeavor, once completed, would increase Maine's hydroelectric output by thousands of kilowatts, regulate and augment the flow of water into more than a half-dozen smaller dams located along the length of the Kennebec, and control flooding.

Working with two other large, growing entities, CMP soon began purchasing, and clearing, parcels in the surrounding area.

Murmurings began among locals, who saw the clearing taking place and hearing the news of their neighbors selling off their land to speculators.

In 1923, the public's fears were realized when a bill was introduced in the state legislature to incorporate the Kennebec Reservoir Company, whose purpose was to dam up the Dead River. A headline from the *Lewiston Journal* in March 1923 reflected public sentiment: "Will the Little Maine Village of Flagstaff Be Wiped Out?"

The contentious bill didn't pass. But anxiety remained—and for good cause. A few years later, the state approved a measure that created the Dead River Storage Company, and the residents of Flagstaff and Dead River learned of their ultimate fate: They were to be flooded, their town taken from them. Also to be doused: The tiny townships of Bigelow and Carrying Place.

Now moving quickly on a project that had been held up by political infighting for more than a decade, CMP had hundreds of workers cutting and clearing trees and burning brush to clear the flowage area. The company began sending letters to residents in affected areas; agents were deployed to go door to door with the somber news.

Hundreds of families, with no other choice, sold their homes and properties, packed up what they could, and left. Some structures were towed away intact to outlying towns such as Eustis. Others, including not only residences but a schoolhouse, Congregational Church, mill, store and Masonic lodge, were dismantled and rebuilt elsewhere. The dead were disinterred and moved to new places of rest, notably Eustis Ridge Cemetery. Businesses took compensation and either folded or relocated. Larger and larger pieces of land came to be owned by CMP.

By November 1949, the waters of Dead River were swallowing up the land, by then largely barren and burned, with a few abandoned buildings and other last vestiges strewn about. The waterway was backing up behind Long Falls Dam, which would be completed in 1950. It took weeks for the waters to creep up over the 20,000 acres of lost towns—an experience that many likened to a slow death.

Now owned and operated by Brookfield Renewable Energy, the dam is a prominent fixture at 45 feet high, 1,339 feet long, with a 450-foot concrete spillway. The reservoir behind it is roughly fifty feet at its deepest.

As Marilyn Rogers-Bull aptly notes in her four-part series in *The Town Line* newspaper on the damming project: "Like all progress, it will not be accompanied without some heartaches."

RAZING LIVES

In 1949, as the lake's waters slowly crept up the landscape toward the ill-fated towns, Flagstaff consisted of about 20 families, many of whom were born there and had always lived there.

Although talk of the damming and reservoir project had been going on for years, they were still stunned by the news that they would soon be homeless.

Many had already moved away to nearby towns. Some, though, refused to give in, resolute to hold out to the bitter, watery end.

Many steadfast residents even continued on with business as usual, holding a regularly scheduled annual town meeting in March. Waterville *Morning Sentinel* columnist Clayton LaVerdiere wrote about the proceedings: "A gallant little town that is slated to die came out with one last, bold gesture of defiance here tonight."

As longtime town clerk Perry Burbank told reporters, "We're still looking ahead as if nothing ever happened."

About thirty Flagstaff voters, many of them "bronzed woods-men and their wives" gathered in the town's tiny schoolhouse "in a businesslike manner that belied the apprehension lurking in the hearts of all." In this, they "studiously avoided discussing the num-bered days of a community that will probably, by next March, be at the bottom of a lake."

Even as hundreds of workers cleared land for the massive project, townspeople voted and appropriated more than $11,000 for twenty-five warrant articles, dropping their ballots into a hat as they had for as long as they could remember. Among their decisions was reelecting Perley Stevens as road commissioner and allocating $1,000 for an "Old Home Day" that many recognized would be a final farewell.

Many, including seventy-six-year-old Captain Cliff Wing, who had lived in town for more than a half-century, lamented of the loss to gathered reporters. Nobody likes being forced from their home; it's simply human nature. "It's just hard to tell where we're going, what we're going to do," said Wing.

The longtime captain and boatsman also made the droll sug-gestion that he could build an ark.

Hilda Ames, who taught many of Flagstaff's roughly forty grammar school, primary school, and high school pupils, agreed that "I've always lived here. It's hard to think of any other place to live."

A woman described as Mrs. Kenneth Taylor—a great-great granddaughter of one of the earliest settlers Rufus Viles—also talked of earlier, happier days, the beauty of which "make us realize (that) our homes here are more precious than ever before."

Letters also inundated local newspapers, with townspeople decrying the loss and saying there could be no compensation. One writer described communities "whose inhabitants live in greater happiness, satisfaction, and far more tranquil peace of mind than . . . harried city folk can imagine."

A FINAL GOODBYE

In the summer of 1949, townspeople did, indeed, hold their Old Home Day, which was covered by newspapers from Maine to Massachusetts. A headline from July 3, 1949 in *The Boston Globe* proclaimed: "Maine Village About to Die Has Farewell Celebration."

Roughly 300 people met in the town, which by then was surrounded by an empty forest, tree stumps, and "a pall of smoke from burning brush" as workers cleared the land of debris to make way for river flowage. The twenty-year-old schoolhouse was being dismantled, its various contents—textbooks, chairs, desks, a radio-phonograph—going to nearby schools or sold to the highest bidder. Many other structures had already been razed or moved, and all those that remained would be flooded. The town outskirts were empty and foreboding.

The two-day community event ended up being a farewell and reunion of sorts, with current and former residents reminiscing about their fond memories of the town and the pleasant times they had there. Rogers-Bull recalled that her family didn't have indoor plumbing or electricity but didn't feel underprivileged; she also described skiing and sliding on Eaton Hill, skating on and swimming in Flagstaff Pond, and many festive school socials and plays.

As reported by *The Morning Sentinel*, the Rev. Arthur R. MacDougall Jr. described the so-called festivities as a solemn Independence Day and a "seeming burial." The eyes of the old were said to be "dimmed with tears." Others questioned what would become of the town's renowned flagstaff, and it was suggested that it be left where it was as an homage to the town and its history.

The flagstaff did stay in place for a time but broke off and fell into the lake. It was salvaged by Captain Wing, who towed it up the lake in his boat and erected it at his new home a half-dozen or so miles from its longtime, original location.

Construction workers were living in abandoned homes; the general store remained open to serve them; the roads were plowed and kept open for the winter; the school bus kept running to carry workers' children to nearby schools. Abandoned dooryards were filled with trucks and machinery, and salvaged lumber was stacked everywhere.

As fate crept over Flagstaff and Dead River like a suffocating shawl, newspapers up and down the coast kept close tabs on events:

"Doomed Town Waits for the End. Uncertain and Thinking of Children. Cord Hanging Over Heads for Over Twenty Years at Last Severed. Area will be Evacuated by Fall. The inhabitants of Flagstaff are watching the flooding. One lady said 'Other towns don't want us, their schools are full, their homes aren't available and where will our men find work? The really old people are the most worried of all, especially about graves.'"

"Creeping, Watery Death to Smother Beauties of Spring in Rural Flagstaff. All Roads are Cut. Residents Gone as Reservoir Grows."

"Dead River, Flagstaff Written Off. Flooded. Hamlets are Legally Dead."

Some "bitter-ended citizens," including Al Wing and Mae Savage, refused to raze or move their homes; they were finally forced to evacuate, the last to leave the condemned town. Black and white photos show their homes half-swallowed in water up to their porches, standing defiant to the bitter end. Consumed by the floodwaters, they eventually broke apart—symbolic images of the town's very end.

In March 1951, once the floodwaters had reached their height, Governor Frederick G. Payne signed two bills surrendering Flagstaff and Dead River. They took effect immediately, and the two towns had not only disappeared—they were officially written off.

A large segment of the displaced population did rebuild a new settlement in Eustis that they named New Flagstaff. Those who know where to look can find remnants of their old buildings—even windows from the church. Families can visit their dead in their new places of rest.

Many remaining survivors—children at the time—describe being "scattered" and, in a sense, untethered. Their family homes are no more; they can't bring their children and grandchildren to even see their general locations because they lie beneath the depths of Flagstaff Lake. Others have decried the sacrilege of having to move their family members' bodies.

Marilyn Rogers-Bull recalled hearing adults talk about the imposing dam and the impending move, and "intolerable" thought. "It was a wonderful place to grow up in," she wrote in *The Town Line*. "Did you ever stop to think what it would be like to not be able to go back to your home-town?"

Today, communities that were once described as "postcard" and "picturesque" are no more. Only water ripples over them, dead towns merely offering ghostly whispers from the deep.

Four

HURRICANE ISLAND

Abandoned Overnight

It was likened by some to the aftermath of Pompeii.

When the once flourishing granite works on Hurricane Island suddenly ceased operations and hundreds of residents hastened for the mainland to find work, the small outcropping off the coast of Vinalhaven, Maine, was left in a sort of suspended animation.

Tools were laid in place where workers had actively been cutting granite just as the final whistle blew; other implements sat waiting to be forged on blacksmith anvils; cutting sheds were full of partially finished blocks that would never be cut into their final, intended shapes.

Company houses overlooking the wharves were even left full of personal belongings: Furniture in sitting rooms, pictures on walls, bowls, plates, and utensils set for a next meal that would never come.

Those who later visited the abandoned island described its aura as eerie, sad, and desolate. Simply put, Hurricane Island had become a ghost town virtually overnight.

A HISTORY FORGED IN GRANITE

Located roughly twelve miles off the rocky western shore of Vinal-haven—today the lobstering capital of Maine—Hurricane Island is a mere mile long and three-quarters of a mile wide. And its geography destined it for its fate: Its core is a massive pillar of granite.

Yet its name is a bit of a mystery: Some purport that "Hurricane" came about because the day it was purchased by George Vinal, a great storm struck. Others say it is on account of its exposed position.

In any case, in 1870 as its industrious fate was initially set, it was spruce covered and wild.

In January of that year, Deborah L. Ginn of Vinalhaven sold the granite isle for $1,000 to a trio of local businessmen: Davis Tillson, Patrick McNamara, and Garrett Coughlin. Tillson, of Rockland, was the driver of the purchase. A West Point graduate and captain in the Civil War, he served in the state legislature as a Republican when the party was yet being formed, and later became adjutant general to Maine.

And he was nothing but a shrewd businessman—as well as a formidable presence despite having had a foot amputated during military service. He found great success in the quarry business, which many credit to his innate engineering abilities.

Also, with the end of the war, there was an increasing desire for granite to support the erection of public buildings and monuments.

All this put Maine, with its large land mass and abundant supply of granite, in a unique position—and Tillson took full advantage.

Still, Philip Conkling of the Island Institute has decried it as "remarkable" how little is known about the great granite period in Maine's history: It spanned more than a century and brought tens of thousands of immigrants to remote island communities to, as he put it, "carve new lives and dreams from cold stone."

Which makes Hurricane Island's story especially poignant: Its quarries weren't as big or as productive as those at nearby Vinalhaven and Mt. Desert, yet it left an impressive, lasting legacy.

ENTERPRISE ABUNDANT

Due both to its ample granite assets and Tillson's business prowess, business did well from the start.

Within just four years, the enterprise was worth $100,000, and the island's sloping hillsides were dotted with roughly fifty dwellings to support a population of between 1,100 and 1,200. Hurricane was developing such a strong reputation that in 1874, former Vice President Hannibal Hamlin (from Paris, Maine) and future U.S. Senator Eugene Hale (from Turner, Maine) paid a visit. And after several years of infighting on the subject, the Maine State Legislature officially incorporated Hurricane Island as its own town in February 1878 (it had previously been part of Vinalhaven).

Throughout the 1870s, steady work for the Hurricane Granite Company came from contracts for state and federal government buildings, post offices, and monuments. Among these were the Library of Congress and the Boston Court House.

The company furnished stone for the Washington Monument; supplied 5,000 tons of paving blocks for the city of Chicago; and its granite was used in the engine house of the Edison Electric Light Station in Brooklyn, the Jersey City Hall, and the Metropolitan Life Insurance Company building in New York City.

To keep things thrumming, stonecutters were recruited from as far away as Ireland, Scotland, Italy, Finland, and Sweden. Worker numbers varied according to available work—anywhere from 400 to 1,000 men whose wages in the 1870s varied from $1 to $3.75 a day. Early on, before workday limits were established, men worked ten-hour days Monday through Friday and nine hours on Saturdays.

As Harold Vinal, a descendant of the island's earliest owners, wrote in his narrative poem, "Hurricane":

And so, they came to Hurricane . . .
the blue-eyed Swedes, the forty dark Italians
with weather-beaten wives and trooping children,
and a mere handful of Americans.

In February 1880, a reporter from the *Rockland Gazette* visited Hurricane to report on the day-to-day goings-on, both from an industrial and a worker's life perspective. (And he painted quite the rosy picture.)

His article described a massive quarry six feet high and 200 feet long. Blasting occurred there roughly once an hour until 4 p.m., when it ramped up to once every two minutes as the working day drew to a close.

The busy operation included six sheds for hammering and chiseling work; "large and suitable" blacksmith shops with twenty-five anvils; a machine shop with trip hammers, metal planers, lathes, and forges; an engine house with two, eighty horsepower boilers; and a workshop for ornamental work. There was also a polishing mill with three large lathes capable of holding columns weighing up to ten tons, and a stationary engine with a massive crane that could take up blocks of twenty tons or more.

To keep everything humming along, railway tracks were laid around the island; these allowed steam cars to carry stone from the quarry for finishing, then down to the wharf to be loaded into large schooners for transport to Boston or New York City. The shed where stone was cut was even curved to allow engines to pass right through it.

As the local newspaper the *Echo* described it: "Perhaps the busiest and most crowded corner of Maine, and will be for some time, is Hurricane Island. It may be safely assumed that no town in New England of its size will present a more busy future than this thriving place."

Still, it wasn't without its strife. There was many an accident, from piston rods catching hold of hands, to the giant blocks the men worked with every day breaking ankles and legs or pinning prone bodies against walls.

Workers eventually formed several unions, including the Granite-Cutters' Union, the Paving Cutters' Union, and the Quarry Workers' Union. These negotiated reduced workdays (nine instead of ten hours during the week and eight instead of nine hours on Saturdays). Then there was the so-called Great Lockout of 1892, a labor strike and walkout that spanned the eastern seaboard.

Tillson, for his part, ever the demanding military captain and politician, was referred to as "Lord of the Isles" by Scottish granite workers, and "Bombasto Furioso" by Italian quarrymen. It was also rumored that during one election he ordered his men to vote Republican (or else). When this was met with strong opposition, he purportedly replied, "I own this island and will be master here."

Local papers, divisive then as now, either lauded or praised him. The Pro-labor *Rockland Opinion* newspaper considered him an oppressor, while the pro-management *Rockland Gazette* saw him as the creator of a utopian community.

ISLAND LIFE

In any case, the island was populous, even boisterous, at times, as reported by local news reports.

At its height, it was a true, free-standing community, with a company office, post office, market, a half-dozen three-story boarding houses, and several other residential dwellings. The boarding houses could accommodate fifty to sixty workers, while houses were rented from the company.

Meanwhile, the ship *Pioneer* made daily trips for those workers who lived on other islands.

Few people on Hurricane owned their own homes, and in fact, it was reported that most workers' paychecks were deposited directly into housing funds or accounts at the local store. This added to some perceptions from outliers of Tillson's authoritarian reputation—as did a strict ban on alcohol. Anyone found drinking this "great enemy of the working man," as reported by the *Rockland Gazette*, was immediately deposed. (Although this ban was purportedly lifted in 1895).

Fifteen wells supplied water for the island; only a couple of houses were fortunate enough to have wells in their cellars. So, until 1909, when the island began shipping in drinking water from Rockland, Hurricane women and children spent a great deal of time transporting water while men worked the quarry and tannery operations.

Still, Hurricaners were said to make the best of their environs, their immigrant populations adopting embellishments from their homelands: chromos, steel engravings, frescoed ceilings, and oil paintings. In their spare time, island sculptors chiseled small decorative statues. The *Gazette* also described the "omnipresent sewing machine," as well as many books, magazines, newspapers, and musical instruments including organs and pianos.

As the newspaper gushed: "You will find in these little dwellings more useful, ornamental and tasteful work scattered around on mantles and brackets, giving evidence of a greater average taste among the people than is found in general society of the same standing."

While the outsides of dwellings might have seemed plain, inside there was singing and "sunny spots where friends linger and lovingly dwell," the reporter continued. "The fact is, the people on the island, both at the public and private table, know how to live; and they live well up to their knowledge."

As Hurricane continued to prosper, the company regularly improved the community, adding a barber shop, enhancing public ways with walks and streetlamps, and renovating the main wharf. A hotel was also built, and its capacity soon increased to accommodate more visitors and boarders.

At the island's most prominent point, meanwhile, there was a large two-story building dedicated to public purposes. Its first floor was devoted to schooling; in 1879, there were a reported sixty-nine scholars who attended classes nine months a year. In 1880, it was reported that Hurricane spent more on their school than any other town in the state ($9.97 per pupil; the next highest was Muscle Ridge, at $2.89).

Former resident Minnie Vinal recalled learning a range of subjects, including reading, writing, figuring, geography, algebra, and bookkeeping. She also described one of the teachers as "part genius and part missionary," and able to teach "any subject to students ranging in age from five to eighteen."

The public building had a recitation room, large hall, library, and permanent stage, a prized Mason and Hamlin Organ, as well; these were used for interdenominational church services, choir recitals, lectures, general gatherings, and adult night classes.

And in 1900, the Archdiocese of Portland saw it fit to build a "mission church" on the island. It was outfitted with stained glass, the cross atop it was gilded with gold, and its proudest possession was a small white cabinet that graced its altar. It was said to have been blessed by the Pope and was brought back from Italy by an island resident. Priests were sent from the mainland on a monthly basis—and in fact, the first service was held in memory of President William McKinley when he was assassinated in 1901.

As for public entertainment? There was plenty. Dances, including an annual "White Duck Ball" for which everyone donned white, were held regularly, and residents from other islands and even the mainland ferried in to attend. There were also dancing classes; as the December 1, 1887, edition of the Vinalhaven *Echo* announced: "Dancing school tonight. Don't forget your white shirts, boys."

Meanwhile, traveling theater troupes and their old-fashioned melodramas came to visit, and island men bowled and played pool and a shuffleboard-like game known as "roller ball."

One of the most festive occasions, though, was a band formed by Italian residents: Every Saturday evening they would dress in native costumes and march the island playing mandolins, guitars, and concertinas. Eventually an amicably dueling band of "Yanks" formed their own musical ensemble that would proceed from the opposite direction, the two meeting to play in unison.

Ultimately, as the newspaper the *Echo* proclaimed: "Long live and prosper little Hurricane, for its inhabitants are the most pleasant people on earth."

AN ABRUPT END

All this seemed to indicate that Hurricane's community and industry would be there to stay for years to come. In 1903, Tom Murphy, the branch secretary of the Granite Cutters' Union, even called conditions in "about the busiest I have any recollection of in the granite industry."

Still, by the early twentieth century, the seeds of its ruin began to germinate. Fissures were caused by the island's dependence on one industry, tradition of strict company government, and lack of private land ownership. Even more so, by 1905, architectural styles began to change with the development of concrete and the concurrently increasing costs of cutting and shipping granite. As a result, there were slowdowns, company restructures, and brief shifts in ownership.

As it was said, one major factor that kept the company going was its superintendent John T. Landers. A longtime town selectman who was well-schooled—attending courses at the Massachusetts Institute of Technology and Rockland Commercial College—he was a continued source of inspiration for workers and refused to give up on island operations.

Still, even he couldn't stem the (literal) tides. The final toll for Hurricane was the sinking of a ship in its harbor on November 8, 1914. The vessel was bound for Rockport, Massachusetts, with a load of 1,200 tons of granite for a breakwater. This massive cargo securely pinned her. And, as often was the case in those days, the ship was not insured.

As a further blow, just about two weeks later, Landers died in Rockland of typhoid fever. He was just forty-six. Company officials could not imagine anyone else taking his place.

The very next morning, drilling and blasting stopped, and the engines at the polishing plant ground to a halt. Workers and residents alike were gathered and told that work would be permanently suspended. Making haste, and having perhaps sensed their fate, Hurricane's families boarded ships for the mainland, never to return, leaving behind possessions too bulky or expensive to transport.

Again, from Harold Vinal's poem:

The marble has turned back to sleep again,
the hammers in the wind at last are silent . . .
The mouse is absent and the swallow gone;
only the indefatigable spider
is nimble with his business. What a pomp,
so fierce to bloom, so quickly to be dust!

A scant few remained behind, notably the Philbrook family, to dismantle buildings and pile their materials by the pier. They lamented to a *Boston Post* reporter in 1916 of the marriages, funerals, and christenings that had all taken place there—the happy and sad times alike, and the sheer loneliness that had replaced them. And yet they held onto the idea that concrete would go out of fashion and granite would experience a revival—the enduring, yet often pitiless, hope of the human spirit.

ECHOES OF PROSPERITY

And while such hope may have faded with time, memories and passed-down reminiscences linger.

Author Eleanor Motley Richardson, who wrote the definitive account, *Hurricane Island: The Town That Disappeared* visited many times over the years and recalled her first trek to the island at age five. It was a picnic and walk with her family, and she described the remnants and fragments of granite blocks strewn about and distinct fence posts marking off the churchyard.

Conkling, for his part, spent years cataloging the natural history of Hurricane Island and other surrounding isles, and has described "archaeological troves" of blocks, columns, monuments, plinths, paving stones, and rusted machinery dotting its sloping cliffs—most being overtaken by flowers, berries, and spruce and alder thickets. Cut into the bedrock, he also found a network of wells and drainage channels that seemed to reveal a complex water works system.

Still, in the end, Hurricane Island's demise isn't wholly unique. As Conkling goes on to explain: "All around the globe are thousands of small islands where people arrived to begin new lives sustained by little more than the fragile offerings of all remote islands. Some colonies have succeeded, but the record, if someone has kept one, would show what a vast number of island communities—often entire cultures—have simply disappeared."

More than a century later, though, there is a positive postscript: For several decades, the islet was home to the Hurricane Island Outward Bound School, which hundreds of students would attend every year to learn about natural history, explore the island and other nearby rocky isles, and try their hand at three-day foraging and backcountry camping "solos."

Given the island's history of abandonment, Outward Bound ultimately left Hurricane in 2006 to relocate to the mainland—but today it has once again been repurposed as a home for the nonprofit Hurricane Island Foundation. This launched in 2010 when the Gaston family, who owned the island and wanted to see it put to good use, signed a forty-year lease with the newly formed nonprofit under the direction of Peter Willauer (formerly of Outward Bound).

Now it is a haven for scientists, researchers, and educators to learn and educate others in hands-on fashion about aquaculture and marine biology. This team manages a three-acre scallop and kelp farm north of the island and tends several flower and produce gardens. With a goal to be as sustainable as possible, the nonprofit's main campus—comprised of classroom space and a lab, cabins, wall tents, yurts, a bunk house, galley, and mess hall—is powered by a photovoltaic system, its water is derived from the quarry pond by way of a solar pump system, and heat for water and comfort comes from solar thermal evacuated tube collectors and back-up propane systems. As much as possible is composted, and greywater is treated and dispersed through a constructed wetland.

So, in a sense, in the twenty-first century, Hurricane Island is going through constant rebirth.

FIVE

MALAGA ISLAND

A Community Exiled

THEY SUDDENLY SHOWED UP ONE DAY: REPRESENTATIVES OF THE state, men in crisp suits and hats, skeptically touring the simple island community, its patchwork homes and unrefined residents.

Then, mere weeks later, another entourage arrived to deliver the news: Vacate the island. Take your possessions. Move your homes if you wanted to or could; otherwise they would be razed. You weren't the state or the public's problem anymore. You were a drain on society, a burden, an embarrassment.

Oh—and you had less than a year to get out.

In 1912, a community of a few dozen men, women, and children with decades of Maine ancestral roots were forced off Malaga Island in Casco Bay simply for being mixed-race and poor. It was a decision made by the state amidst ongoing racism, nativism, classism, since debunked concepts about interbreeding and shifting economic factors.

Today, the island is a public preserve and critical historic site—and the story of its despicable history has ebbed and flowed, has been engulfed, and has resurfaced. And more than one hundred years later, it remains one of the darkest blots on Maine's storied history.

THRIVING ON DIVERSITY

Malaga is a roughly forty-acre irregular oval heaving out of the ocean in Casco Bay north of Portland. It is sheltered between the mainland town of Phippsburg and the larger Bear Island, near the mouth of New Meadows River.

As was the case with many of the thousands of islands scattered along the Maine coast, it was initially inhabited by natives—within the last 1,000 years, as determined by archaeologists. It wasn't until 1818 that it came into formal possession of local settlers: Eli Perry, one of the first residents of Phippsburg, purchased it for $150. Although there is no evidence that Perry or his ancestors ever paid taxes on the property, the family plays an integral role in the tragic demise of the Malagan community.

That story goes back to Benjamin Darling, an Amerindian slave who arrived in Maine in the late 1700s with a Captain Darling. The seafarer immigrated to the states to help establish a saltworks in Phippsburg. So, the story goes, in 1794, Benjamin was granted his freedom after saving his master's life in a shipwreck. He was also granted a reward that he used to buy Horse Island (present-day Harbor Island) at the mouth of New Meadows River not far from Malaga. He married a white woman and was said to be ever loyal to his former master, putting in hard work at the salt factory. Remaining stories (or legends) about him are colorful; in one he was apparently mauled by a bear while trying to defend his neighbor's corn patch.

His descendants moved out to various islands throughout the surrounding bay, including Malaga. The isle's first known settler was Henry Griffin, who established a homestead on its east side in the mid-1800s. The island was as yet unnamed, and it has been suggested that "Malaga" was to honor Captain Darling's wrecked brig—and Benjamin's resultant freedom—because it was purportedly loaded with timber from Malaga, Spain. A small, multiracial, working-class community soon established itself, largely comprised of Darlings and Griffins and their progeny, people who had decades of ancestral roots in Maine. By 1880, Malaga had twenty-seven residents; by 1900, there were forty.

The island served as a refuge of sorts for poorer fishing families who couldn't afford the rising cost of coastal real estate. Residents lived in meager, one-room and tarpaper shacks constructed from local timber and other materials they could come by. Some made use of discarded shells as foundations. Islanders relied on local resources to sustain themselves: catching groundfish, netting bait-fish, digging clams, lobstering, hunting local fowl. Much like the natives who had come before them, they also foraged for berries and other edible vegetation and maintained modest gardens of beans, corns, and potatoes. Some worked at mainland resorts and larger farms or took in laundry from Phippsburg and other nearby towns as trade for more substantial provisions. Still, it often wasn't enough. By the turn of the century, a "pauper relief" fund from Malaga's parent town of Phippsburg helped islanders survive, particularly in the winter.

Around the same time, news of the island and its purportedly destitute, financially struggling, under-educated residents began to spread—and on a wider scale. Moved by their Christian duty, missionaries George and Lucy Lane came to Malaga in the summer months to teach island children basic literacy, mathematics, "domestic science," social graces, and hygiene. And religious values, of course. All this to help them advance their ranks to middle-class respectability. With help from the Malaga Island Settlement Association, church groups, businesses, and other locals, they eventually built the island's first (and as it would turn out, only) schoolhouse, a one-room structure overlooking the bay. They also enlisted young women to provide year-round instruction.

Given its strong financial backing and the earnest efforts of the Lanes, the Malaga Island School was considered by some to be better than many around—at least one mainlander was said to have paid to have their child attend. A pamphlet for backers, *History of Lane's School*, included "before and after" pictures to illustrate its success. This included a black child, Abbie, first posed in an image seated on an old woman's lap—face dirty, hair tangled, simple cotton frock soiled. It was accompanied with an "as she is now" shot of her scrubbed up, hair smoothed, donning a clean school dress. Newspaper reports from the time praised the missionaries' efforts, describing "cleanly dressed children who, a year ago, could not read or write," but who could now "read short sentences, count, spell, and do some excellent written exercises." They were also called "fully as bright as the whites and fully as eager to learn." *The Boston Journal*, for its part, reported that the school "contained the one bright gleam of civilization in the entire colony."

PREJUDICE: INJUSTICE

But even as the Lanes and their supporters were making such inroads, larger forces were at work. The general sentiment came to be that Malaga should be cleansed, on both a literal and figurative scale.

The expansion of railroads and an increase in steamship building impacted Maine's longtime economic backbone, wooden shipbuilding. Fishing and lobstering industries were suffering due to decreased stocks (the result of decades of over-catching). Phippsburg, as a result, was suffering from outmigration, and there was local backlash against aid for the poor outliers.

The state grasped on a new industry that would save it: tourism. (And as the decades have shown us, in the end, that bet was right.) But Malaga and the deplorable state of its residents and their homes was a blight; it discouraged and offended wealthy summer visitors and spoiled their views of the bay and the Atlantic. Also, should it be cleared of its residents and ramshackle structures, perhaps it could be made into a resort that contributed rather than detracted from Phippsburg's coffers.

As one writer described it: "But enough of this poor colored race, we doubt not many of them have white hearts." If the "spot of natural beauty" and "gem of an isle" could be depopulated and rebuilt, "what a change and what an imposing entrance to our beautiful New Meadows River."

Then there were the overarching racial sentiments that prevailed even in the northeast—which typically prided itself on its progressiveness in that area during the Civil War and the years following. Segregation and racial violence were rampant, and then came the Supreme Court ruling in 1896 that upheld Jim Crow laws and their "separate but equal" doctrine. And finally, eugenics, a growing belief that racial intermingling resulted in "undesirable traits" including ignorance, criminality, and sexual immorality. Miscegenation, or interbreeding, was outlawed in twenty-nine states, with many holding to the concept that racial intermingling threatened the social order. Charles Davenport, a prominent eugenicist from Connecticut, argued that "defective" people including "idiots, low imbeciles, incurable and dangerous criminals" be prevented from procreation by either segregation or sterilization. Following this precept, many states, including Maine, established so-called Schools for the Feebleminded, where "decaying stock" were locked away and thus removed from society.

Amidst all this, Phippsburg got into a several-year feud with nearby Harpswell over which town owned Malaga. The state eventually came into possession of the island, leaving residents wards of Maine under the jurisdiction of the Governor's Executive Council.

All the while, local, regional, and eventually national newspapers resorted to rumor and fearmongering. They held up Malaga—dirty, primitive, poor, multiracial—as a prime example of what could happen with interbreeding. Racist postcards were even circulated as far south as Boston. These depicted two shy children in filthy, unkempt clothing and a dour-faced elderly woman apparently recreated in a mud-filled animal pen behind a dilapidated structure. The images are believed to be staged.

Numerous other pictures from the early 1900s depict children, black and white together, sometimes barefoot and wearing mismatched clothing, striking tentative poses; students, boys in suspenders, white shirts and newsboy hats, girls in modest dresses, lined up outside school; laundry hanging out to dry, dories hauled up on the beach, families gathered in front of their homes, going about their everyday lives. Photographers also captured the quaint new schoolhouse with its precipitous set of steps leading up from the beach; slope-roofed tarpaper shacks and other makeshift structures hewn together with uneven clapboards and scraps of wood; the island's scattering of mismatched homes juxtaposed against the sturdier Colonials and Capes across the bay in mainland Phippsburg.

At the time before their exile, the families here were Murphys, Dunnings, Johnsons, and Marks. James McKenney, a Phippsburg native of Scotch-Irish descent, was known informally as the "King of Malaga" because he was de facto spokesman and community leader. It was at his home that Malaga's children were taught by the Lanes prior to the building of the schoolhouse in 1909. John Eason was also a well-known and respected figure on the island; a master carpenter and mason, he was known as "the deacon" because he conducted religious services on Malaga when bad weather kept people from attending church on the mainland. Then there was

Eliza Griffin, a progressive sort who headed her own household and made more money than any man on the island by working as a fisherwoman, laundress, and housekeeper.

Still, the wider public hardly saw these images or heard the islander's personal stories. Instead, "Malagaites" were described as ex-slaves or offspring of slaves or concubines, a heathen, degraded, unnatural mix of blacks and whites who had children out of wedlock. They were predisposed to alcoholism, crime, poverty, laziness, mental deficiency, and immorality, and they abhorred soap and cleanliness. Some rumors even circulated about island children living in tunnels and growing horns from staying in the dark too long.

An article from the *Bath Enterprise* condemned Malaga as a "godless island," while the *Casco Bay Breeze* described it as "the home of southern negro blood," with "incongruous scenes on a spot of natural beauty in Casco Bay."

Under the headline, "Not Fit for Dogs. Life on Malaga," the *Boston Transcript* proclaimed: "Poverty, immorality and disease. Disgusting and pitiable. A population of 35, and 26 of them sick with measles. No food, no beds, no fuel and scant shelter all winter long. Ignorance, shiftlessness, filth and heathenism. A shameless disgrace that should be looked into at once. The town of Phippsburg disowns these creatures and they are made outcasts."

Even as late as the mid-century, the *Lewiston Evening Journal* perpetuated racist sentiments, describing Malaga as a sacrilegious place where it was commonplace to see a "renegade white for a father; a fat frau black as night for a mother; three children all white the offspring! What a blood endowment for the youngster."

BANISHMENT

Finally, bowing to public pressure, newly elected Maine Governor Frederick Plaisted toured the island with a fellow group of state officials on July 11, 1911. He met with residents, inspected their homes, and was serenaded with a hymn by students of the school-house. While he praised the school, Plaisted later told the *Bruns-wick Record* that "the people cannot be forced to leave their poor homes, and we must not encourage others to go there."

Officials met to discuss the situation and the costs of public assistance. Governor's Council minutes describe Malaga and other poor towns including Frenchboro and Athens as a "blot upon the state" and a "drain on the treasury." Supporting them simply encouraged paupers to attract "a thriftless, lazy gang, to help them in consuming supplies furnished by the Commonwealth."

Still, upon learning that the state could not evict the islanders itself, Plaisted instructed the Maine Attorney General to find a legal owner who could. The ensuing finding was that Eli Perry's heirs were rightful owners. Within three weeks of the governor's visit, the family issued eviction orders to the "Malagaites"—a term then and now considered a slur. They had until July 1, 1912, to vacate the island. They could remove their homes and possessions, but anything that remained on eviction day would be razed or burned. This to prevent disgraced residents from returning to and recolonizing the island.

After the notices were handed out, the state purchased the island from the Perrys for $471 and agreed to pay nominal sums (pittances really) to some families if they left promptly and quietly. "I think the best plan would be to burn down the shacks with all of their filth," Plaisted was reported saying at the time. "Certainly, the conditions there are not credible to our state. We ought not to have such things near our front door."

The ensuing eviction procedures included assessments of each resident's household, as well as their physical, mental, and financial conditions. As a result, roughly a half-dozen residents were deemed "feeble minded." This included most of the Marks family, including father Jacob, Mother Abbie, son James, daughters Lizzie, Lottie, and Eta, and grandson William.

The entire family was considered unfit for society and thus suitable for incarceration, and they were taken to the Maine School for the Feeble-Minded in New Gloucester. At the time, all it took to be committed was a standard form with a physician's signature and approval from a sheriff and probate judge. The fill-in-the-blank certificate for the Marks states that family members were not necessarily candidates for an "insane hospital," but they were proper subjects for the feeble-minded school. This decision was based in part on their failure of a so-called clinical test that involved identifying modern inventions such as the telephone (which had not yet arrived on the island). Upon reaching the institution, the family was split up, and Jacob and James died not long thereafter. Others who were carted off for incarceration were purportedly sterilized.

Meanwhile, islanders who escaped that grim fate faced another in impending homelessness. Cast out by society, many spent months looking for new places to live. Some were able to salvage their tumble-down homes and float them to the mainland; a few docked at a landing in Phippsburg that soon bore the crass nickname "N***er Ridge." Of the many heartbreaking stories was that of the Tripps; the family of six tied their shack to a dinghy, but when they attempted to secure a lot to relocate it, they were prevented from doing so several times by spurning locals. When mother Laura became ill, pater familias Robert rowed three miles in a winter storm—but when he returned with a doctor, his wife had died.

Even the community's population of the dead were considered unfit to remain on the island: They were dug up, transported to the mainland and reinterred on the grounds of the state-run institution in New Gloucester. Many are believed to have been shoveled into large communal plots. Today that property is Pineland Farms, a 5,000-acre recreation area, event venue and working farm; here, too, the evicted islanders remain in relative obscurity, shaded away by trees and memorialized with a simple plaque. Some of their descendants lay there, as well, because local churches aware of their ancestry refused their burial.

So, in roughly a year's time, Malaga was rid of its shunned residents—alive and dead. Any structures that were left behind were taken apart. The new schoolhouse, which had been in use for just three years, was moved to Louds Island in Muscongus Bay, where it was repurposed as a church. The state then sold the island to Everard A. Wilson, who had close ties to Plaisted's Executive Council charged with investigating conditions on Malaga. The plans to build a summer resort on the isle never amounted to anything.

For years, newspaper accounts continued to laud the expulsion; it was considered a great success not only for Maine but "the cause of humanity." The island had been returned to its natural pristinity, the state was no longer financially responsible for its derelict population, and the "unfit" who promoted immorality and caused bad publicity had been institutionalized.

One headline from 1913 proclaimed, "Cleaning up Malaga Island—No Longer a Reproach to the Good Name of the State." Another article from the following year made the racially charged and metaphoric statement that "the dark spots are gradually being whitened."

Other reports went so far as to call it a positive for the evicted, as well—they experienced little hardship and would have better lives because of it. "Not only have the inhabitants of the island been raised to a standard of living they have probably never dreamed of before, but the state had saved a little bundle of coin as well," one newspaper assented.

ONE HUNDRED YEARS LATER, AN APOLOGY

In the many decades that followed, with the island barren of human inhabitants, Malaga became a dirty secret—both for those with connections to it and those who had shunned them. Resettled islanders and their ancestors worked to forge new lives and identities in a society that had so dramatically spurned and maligned them. Many hid their connections to the island or refused to acknowledge them.

Marnie Darling Voter, for one, a descendant of Benjamin Darling who has been outspoken in the press about the despicable exile of Malaga's residents, recalls discovering her ancestry in the 1970s. But when she approached her father about the news, he turned to her sternly and ordered her to stop, and to never speak of it again, lest he disown her.

"Malagaite" remained a slur and a label no one wanted to bear— or hear. Simply put, it was considered a "story best left untold."

And for many years, it was. Lottie Marks Blackwell, one of the last living residents of Malaga, died in 1997 at age 103. As has often been the case throughout history, little remains of the oppressed; there are no known remaining letters, diaries, or other writings from residents. History has not told their side of the story. And a further tragedy is that now, as people begin to reexamine what happened there, there is no one left to tell—only bits and pieces of oral histories (if any) have been passed down. One can only imagine the helplessness and despair islanders felt as they were so crudely displaced and scorned.

The island itself changed ownership several times over the next eighty-plus years, but no significant structures were built there; it was largely used to store fishing gear and traps until its purchase in 2001 by Maine Coast Heritage Trust.

But time began to erode that shame and stigma and people started talking frankly about Malaga. This came with changing perspectives on race and history and more nuanced approaches to both. The island's deplorable story allowed for a larger discussion on racism and classism, particularly as it pertained to turn-of-the-century New England, which always prided itself on its abolitionism and supposed inclusiveness. Historians and archaeologists have been digging (both literally and figuratively) into that past; writers and artists alike have explored it through words and imagery. One such example is African American artist Daniel Minter of Georgia; he incorporates vintage photographs and artifacts such as buttons (from a small laundry business that operated on the island) into his work. Threaded throughout his paintings and assemblage are figures cupping their hands around their cores—a signification that, no matter what else, some things simply can't be taken away from people.

There's a somber reality amidst continued racial tensions, he has told reporters. "It's really important that Malaga is not forgotten because it could so easily, easily happen again," he said in an interview with Spectrum Local News.

Still, even as people begin to revisit its plight, the first formal apology didn't come until 2010—nearly one hundred years after its community was evicted. On April 7, 2010, on the final day of the session of the Maine state legislature, representatives unanimously passed a resolution expressing "profound regret" over the islander's "tragic displacement."

Later that year, then-Governor John Baldacci and other state politicians gathered with ancestors in an emotional ceremony on the shores of Malaga. "To the descendants of Benjamin Darling, let me just say that I'm sorry," he said to the assembled crowd, many of whom wiped tears from their eyes. "I'm sorry for what was done. It wasn't right and we were raised better than that. We're better people than that." He continued: "It's reprehensible what happened to your families. The spirit you bring today is a spirit that others can learn from. Because it isn't about retribution and revenge and hate and violence. It's about trying to find hope and opportunity."

Herb Adams, a professor of history and government and the representative who drafted the state legislature's resolution, offered the eulogy: "Peace, at last to Malaga. May scientists explore its secrets. May students study its histories. May Mother Nature reclaim her own. And may the old ghosts find peace at last."

In 2017, the memorial was erected at Pineland Farms, and the state has also created a college scholarship for Malaga's descendants. Maine Coast Heritage Trust has welcomed continued archaeological excavation and field research on Malaga. Researchers have studied shell midden deposits and conducted surveys of tidal flats and have recovered roughly 50,000 artifacts. These have included ceramics, pipe stems, leather, nails, fishhooks, and coins dating from the 1880s to 1912, the year the community formally ceased to be. They have also discovered foundation holes, stone-lined wells, and shell midden deposits that represent historic waste dumps and foundation sites. Interpretive programs are held periodically, and the island is open to daytime recreation.

Today, the historic site and wildlife habitat is comprised of a spruce-fir forest, meadows, brackish ponds, salt marshes, and narrow, rocky-shored beaches. Local fishermen and lobstermen still store their traps and other gear on the isle, a continued symbol of Maine's maritime heritage. Although there is no public transportation to the island, visitors are welcome to land small boats and explore; a one-mile loop trail traverses Malaga and a self-guided tour passes the former site of the schoolhouse, as well as the McKenney, Marks, Griffin, and Eason homesteads and stone-lined wells that provided residents with water.

It is a beautiful, pastoral locale. But it is also one with ghostly, mournful reminders of human oppression and hatred—and a plea to learn from, and not repeat, the past.

Six

SWAN ISLAND/PERKINS

Ghost Isle

AFTER DEBOARDING THE DOCKED FERRY OR DRAGGING YOUR canoe or kayak onto the sand-and-reed covered shore, you have your choice of nature trails threading through pastoral landscapes; past marshland, duck ponds, and cove and island views; down gravel roads lined with trees left alone to grow in their enormous splendor.

And suddenly you come upon them: eighteenth and nineteenth century houses spotting the landscape. Clearly vacant and largely left to the elements, some are weather-beaten and sagging, others uniquely oh-so-New-England architectural.

Today, the former village of Perkins—a tiny slice of an island four miles long and vacillating between one-half and three-quarters of a mile wide depending on tidal levels—is known as Swan Island and is a National Historic Register Historic District, recreation destination, and wildlife management area.

But its pristine presence belies its historically rich, often tumultuous past: early stoppers-by who became renowned to history; numerous native attacks; eventual settlement by residents who prospered in numerous livelihoods.

And with a half-dozen structures and two cemeteries still remaining, it is an abandoned town truly frozen in time.

EUROPEAN ARRIVAL

Located in the Kennebec River between the towns of Richmond and Dresden at the head of Merrymeeting Bay, Swan is one of two islands bearing its name off the coast of a state renowned for its hundreds of islets, archipelagos, and peninsulas. The other juts out of the Atlantic off Mount Desert Island on Maine's northern coast.

And as tends to be the case with many islands in Maine—due to its shifting populations from natives to infringing white settlers—the origin of the Swan name is up for conjecture. Once believed to be a summer locale for native Abenaki people, it may have originally been called "Swango"—which translates to "island of eagles." This is due to its high and varied population of the large birds of prey. Another theory is that it was given its "Swan" title because those large, snowy white, graceful creatures purportedly frequented it on their migrations north and south. (However, many historians and wildlife experts alike have refuted this idea, especially as swans are not known to migrate.) Swan's northern name partner, meanwhile, honors Colonel James Swan of Fife, Scotland, who is credited with organizing the colonization of the island and other surrounding areas in the eighteenth century.

The first recorded European visit (or at least sail-by) of the future Perkins/Swan was in 1605 during an expedition under the prolific explorer Samuel de Champlain. Coursing up the Kennebec, they had been sent from the struggling St. Croix Island settlement to find potential alternatives for a permanent colony. Two years later, Champlain drafted a map of so-called New France that depicted the river and its several large islands. That same year, the English established what goes down in the history books as either Popham Colony or Sagadahoc Colony at the mouth of the Kennebec—their first effort to obtain permanent settlement in New England.

A party from the colony led by Raleigh Gilbert—son of the distinguished Humphrey Gilbert, an explorer and soldier who claimed Newfoundland for England and died in the service of Queen Elizabeth I—soon sailed upriver as far as modern-day state capital Augusta. Passing Swan Island both upriver and downriver, their official report was that: "We fynd this ryver to be very pleasant with many goodly Illands." The legendary Captain John Smith then reportedly dropped in on the isle (which then still had a healthy population of natives) in 1614.

Swan officially enters the deed books in 1667 when the Abbagassets and Kennebes sold it to Christopher Lawson. The prominent Boston entrepreneur and land agent was the first settler to build a home on the island, where he lived for a few years. But by the 1680s, Swan had transferred hands a few times and became just another land holding—one of many being prolifically gobbled up by encroaching Europeans.

TRAGEDY STRIKES AND HISTORY PASSES

With this encroachment came decades of strife: Beginning in 1675, the New England colony was ravaged by decades of Frontier (or Indian) Wars—despite the establishment of several forts up and down coastal and inland waterways, including Fort Richmond near the western edge of the Kennebec opposite Swan Island.

The first non-native homesteader, Thomas Percy, set up on the island in 1730. But he remains but a footnote in Swan's history. It was the purchase of the islet by Captain James Whidden in 1750 that represents the first permanent settlement—permanent as it were, as his family's story had a dreadful end. They had been there but a short time, when, in September 1850, their home was attacked by natives. Whidden and his wife were able to evade capture by hunkering in the cellar, but their two sons, daughter, son-in-law, seven grandchildren, and two servants were taken hostage. They were then transported to Quebec, where they were sold—all but the youngest granddaughter, who was adopted by a young French couple. So it goes, the adults fetched $29 each; the children barely anything.

Despite her desire to stay with her foster parents, the youngest girl was returned to Swan by state officials a few years later as a teenager. Other members of her family also returned to find their birth mother had died, and that the once venerable captain was living in filth and poverty.

Put perhaps one of Swan Island's most intriguing (and notorious) contributions to history came a half-century later, with the outbreak of the Revolutionary War.

In late 1775, a young Aaron Burr was on duty with Benedict Arnold's troops during the distinguished officer's (ultimately failed) attempt to capture Quebec. As the forces made their way up the Kennebec, they paused for a feast at Fort Western in modern-day Augusta. While there, the future vice president to Thomas Jefferson met Jacataqua, a sachem (or priestess) of an Abenaki tribe then living on Swan Island. She was said to be beautiful, charming, and well-versed in the arts of the wild, even teaching Arnold's men to hunt boar. The two apparently hit it off so well that she followed the troops to Quebec—and soon learned she was pregnant with Burr's child, a baby girl she named Chestnutiana. Let it be known that deeper delving by historians has also revealed that the notorious womanizer Burr sired several illegitimate children with local native girls, a fact he either never knew or acknowledged.

In any case, Burr brought Jacataqua back to New York and set her up in a cabin on Long Island. And (as legend says anyway) when Burr shot and killed Alexander Hamilton in their controversial duel in 1804, Jacataqua was so distressed that she threw herself into New York's East River. Stories also purport that when the financially ruined and ostracized Burr suffered a stroke and was resigned to live out his life in a boardinghouse, Chestnutiana came to her father's side to tend to him.

Whatever the truth, the story adds to Swan Island's enduring allure.

THE TIDES TURN

By the mid-1700s, as the danger of Indian attacks decreased, Swan once again attracted settlers. In 1766 according to Census records, eighteen residents were recorded on the island.

That population only continued to grow, as Swan was in a prime location to contribute to several flourishing economies, including fishing of local shad, lumbering, and farming. Notably, it became locally renowned for its ice harvesting (three major ice houses once operated on the island) and its shipbuilding (at least seven oceangoing vessels were built there).

But until the mid-1800s, it was still under the purview of the town of Dresden, which levied high taxes. In 1847, despite years of opposition from this "mother town" that didn't want to lose that influence (or tax revenue), Swan seceded and became Perkins. Unlike "Swan," the origins of this name are clear: It was to honor Col. Thomas Handasyd Perkins, Jr., a wealthy China merchant credited with helping establish the original township. He is also more widely known as the patron of the Perkins School for the Blind in Watertown, which was founded in 1829.

From then on, the town continued to prosper, building a schoolhouse in the 1850s and an interconnected set of "highways" running across the island. The establishment of White's Landing (present-day Richmond) only contributed to that prosperity, as regular ferry service soon started up between the island and the mainland town. By 1860, Swan's population was 100 residents; in 1900, it was ninety-five (according to respective Census reports).

However, the latter number reflects the beginning of the end of Swan's successful run. Plug-in refrigerators were growing in popularity, thus reducing the need for ice blocks. Iron and steel, rather than wood, became the norm for shipbuilding. Pollution in the Kennebec impacted shad fishing. The island had been largely forested, making lumbering all but impossible.

With their livelihoods in jeopardy, islanders began to filter out of Perkins, and by 1918, with not enough men to fill town offices, Perkins became Perkins Township. And with the onset of the Great Depression in 1929, the island's remaining vestiges of farming suffered, causing further exodus. The final toll of fate rang in 1936, when ferry service from Dresden ceased with the building of a bridge upriver on the Kennebec.

Sensing opportunity, the Maine Department of Inland Fish and Wildlife began purchasing land on Swan in the 1940s. With its abundant fields, remaining woods, and mud flats, the island was an ideal location for migrating the IF&W's production and management of waterfowl such as duck and geese. The state continued to purchase land as it became available, and by the mid-twentieth century, Swan was effectively a ghost town.

EXPLORING—AND PRESERVING—THE PAST

To visit the island now is, in all senses, to be transported back in time.

Thanks to state and federal efforts, it has been preserved for the ages as the Swan Island Wildlife Management Area. Owned and managed by Maine's IF&W, it was designated a National Historic Register Historic District in 1996. It can be accessed via a ferry ride or a short canoe or kayak across the Kennebec, and its narrow length features roughly 900 acres of forestland and 400 acres of open fields, as well as seven miles of hiking trails and a four-and-a-half-mile dirt road. There are also ten Adirondack shelters for camping; these are located overlooking an eighteenth-century field, nearby Little Swan Island, and the eastern channel of the Kennebec. True to its Native American name "Swango," the island continues to be an important breeding area for bald eagles; other species that frequent the island include buteos, falcons, and accipiters, and it is also home to blue herons, deer, turkey, elusive fox, and a menagerie of other wildlife. Visitors can view (or attempt to view) these from the island's wildlife observation tower, which has its own story to tell: It was originally built on Frye Mountain in Montville in 1931 and aided in the prevention and suppression of wildfires until 1991. It was restored and moved to Swan in 2005.

The dirt road that traverses the island hearkens to simpler times. This path takes visitors past not only mixed forest, lush fields, freshwater tidal flats, ponds, and wetlands, but remaining cellar holes, hand-dug wells, two cemeteries, and the half-dozen homes that remain.

Notable among these is the circa-1800 Tubbs-Reed house, tucked away among a thicket of giant trees. From a distance, two of its front windows are obscured by a blunted arbor as if it's tentatively peering out from its long silence. The square, Federal-style house features rounded interior corners, floor stenciling, and is outfitted with a Dutch oven and antiques from Perkins, including a spinning wheel and bed. It was built by Samuel Tubbs, a major in the Massachusetts militia during the American Revolution. As was a regular practice at the time, he was reportedly granted the land as reward for his service. The house was restored in 1968 and is now maintained by the state and the Friends of Swan Island.

Nearby, the 1763 Gardiner-Dumaresq saltbox sits stately on an open hill. Its name reflects its architectural design, as it features a dramatically sloping roof due to its two stories in the front and one in the rear. The house was built by Bostonian Dr. Sylvester Gardiner as a summer residence for his daughter Rebecca and her husband Philip Dumaresq and has quite the colorful history of its own. A loyalist, Dumaresq was forced into exile in the West Indies following the American Revolution. The couple's son eventually came into possession of the property, but after returning from a trip to Gardiner in 1826, his boat sunk, and he drowned. His son Philip then took over the estate as a summer residence—but in a related tragedy in 1855, his wife, daughter, and a friend drowned while swimming in Little River. A few years later, while on Long Island Sound, Philip himself was then lost overboard and drowned. Eventually ending this series of dreadful events, the state purchased the property in the 1940s, restored it in the 1960s with federal funding and still maintains it in conjunction with the Friends of Swan Island. Its adjacent, 100-year-old boathouse is used for wildlife and conservation programming and workshops.

The circa-1850 Maxwell-Tarr House also remains, yet unmaintained. This fact is clear in its appearance: It has been withered and sagged by the years, and its entry door has lost its accompanying front steps. A simple, traditional New England Colonial house, the property it sits on was one of the last active farms on the island. The existing 1886 Robinson-Powell House, paint stripped off by the years, outbuildings sagging and mold-covered, well pump jutting from the backyard, is used as an occasional residence by summer employees. Of particular intrigue is Curtis Cemetery, hemmed in by an uneven whitewashed fence, stones subtly heaved upwards or sideways or pulled down by time. These markers range from 1802 to 1968. Traditionally, Maine families maintained separate burial sites, but all except one of the markers was moved here. Although the burial ground was willed to the state in the late 1980s, descendants of Swan Island residents retain rights to it—a final vestige of remembrance.

Remaining, as well, is the town corn crib; its cement legs kept corn away from moisture, their metal tops preventing greedy mice and rats from pilfering its holdings. It also features an air slat screen that helped dry the corn after it was husked and before it was stored as cattle feed in the winter.

Then there are the island's magnificent White Oak trees, which (when allowed) are long-lived and distinctive for their enormous, rounded, bell-like crown. Natives ground their acorns, which are much less bitter than that of the Red Oak, to make crude flour. Swan Island represents the northern edge of their range in Maine.

Ultimately, these stately arbors standing as strong sentinels over the island's architectural artifacts and pristine natural abundances remind us that the past is never truly gone, and there is always a possibility for rebirth.

Seven

RICEVILLE

A Land of Legends

ONE LOCAL YARN HAS IT THAT, AT THE TURN OF THE TWENTIETH century, correspondence, and communication from the small town of Riceville suddenly ceased. Concerned, a couple from a neighboring town ventured into the Hancock County hamlet—and were shocked at what they discovered.

Entering town, they came upon one dead body in the street; continuing on, they found several others felled in the road, around buildings, and out in fields and pastures.

Yet another bit of lore with thin threads of truth says that a trader who regularly visited the village returned one day to find that everyone had simply up and vanished.

Although further probing into the town's seemingly sudden abandonment has revealed much more mundane truths, Riceville has yet prompted many a legend—a town, it was said for decades, that simply disappeared.

Located near present-day Township 39 at the convergence of Penobscot and Hancock counties in Maine's Midcoast, what was once Riceville is now overgrown and mostly lost to the woods; mere tangential echoes remain. But one hundred some-odd years ago, it was a small but bustling community built up around an extensive, busy tannery. This bark extracting operation was located along the banks of Buffalo Stream (a decidedly unusual name for a state that has never been known to be roamed by the giant animals).

The tannery was first purchased by F. Shaw and Brothers Company, a leather-making giant that owned and managed numerous tanneries across the state. The company acquired the site in the 1860s, and it soon comprised of workers' residences, a store, and a post office. By 1890, the community is reported to have been home to 136 residents.

Despite the enterprise's (and the town's) success, though, F. Shaw ran into legal problems in the early 1880s, when a New York City bank demanded repayment of $133,000 for bills receivable and past-due accounts, as well as assets including thousands of cords of bark, leather, hides, and other merchandise. The company's other described assets included the tanneries, extract factories, dwellings, and personal property; a store; 1,500 acres of land, timber rights (known as "stumpages"), railroad cars, vacuum pans, and engines.

In 1898, Hancock Leather Company—consisting of James, John, and Francis X. Rice of Bangor—took over the operations and property. It was then that the town got its official name: Riceville. Under its new ownership, the tannery also changed focus, shifting to manufacturing sole leather by tanning shipped-in raw buffalo hide.

Still, Riceville's prosperity was short-lived, with the hamlet's population declining by nearly half, to seventy-five residents, by 1900. According to research by the group Bangor Ghost Hunters, this population included eleven families, thirty-five children, and eighteen boarders. At the time, the Riceville school was also reported to have an enrollment of twenty-one pupils, these with names including Buck, Cole, Peaterson, Priest, and Willette.

And then on the eve of 1907, final disaster struck: *The Bangor Daily Commercial* reported that, on December 30, the plant at Riceville was "entirely destroyed" by fire. The cause: an exploding lantern in its roll house. The conflagration took down the roll house as well as the large tannery, sawmill, engine and boiler house, and the property's large bark yards. The fire "gained such headway that with the apparatus at hand nothing could be done to save the buildings," as noted in the *Daily Commercial.*

The newspaper further reported that the tannery employed about twenty-five men, and that the general store and boarding house were spared. Hancock Leather began to consider whether to rebuild the plant, "but has reached no conclusion as yet."

Its owners' final resolution should come as no surprise to the reader: The plant was never rebuilt, and residents began filtering out of town to seek viable work elsewhere. By 1910, what had once been Riceville was all but abandoned.

In the hundred years since, as the town and its history have faded from history, rumors have, as they often do, inexplicably abounded. There was the trader who purportedly found the town suddenly deserted; the couple who discovered the bodies strewn about. Other stories were that the town was completely wiped out or abandoned because of a cholera outbreak or due to chemicals from the tannery seeping into the water supply. As it has been rumored, residents from outlying towns then buried the dead in unmarked graves.

This legend and lore are ultimately all that remain. Any memories are kept by the dead, and the town has vanished to mere remnants. Curious history buffs and intrepid ghost hunters have explored the old township by traveling in by all-terrain vehicles then bushwhacking along narrow, dead-ending dirt roads, swamps, and bogs. They have relayed details of deep, yawning, deteriorating cellar holes; sections of former brick ovens and old wood stoves; and debris such as wagon axles, shoes with brass tacks, chunks of metal. One group has even claimed to find the remnants of an old, tanned buffalo hide.

One of the most unique reminders of the town, though, is its perplexing, eerie burial ground—or what once was. A faded wooden sign tacked to a tree identified it as Riceville Cemetery—yet it is merely an uneven oval hemmed in by a dilapidated fence in overgrown woods. It contains no headstones whatsoever.

Ultimately, its unexplained sparseness serves as a fitting testament to the mystery of this mostly forgotten place and the abounding rumors it has since inspired.

Part II

Massachusetts

You set me on a firmly laid and simple course. Then removed the road . . .

—Genesis

Massachusetts is deeply endowed with history, innovation, education, and culture—its nickname "The Hub" is a well-earned one. Not to mention, it is geographically diverse: With its prominent head, crooked arm and elbow and rectangular body, its 10,555 square miles range from wooded wilds, to ocean coastlines and beaches, to rivers and lakes, to open land and metropolises.

Reflecting this history and diversity but belying its size, the state has a surprising number of ghost towns and abandoned villages— from the very tip of Cape Cod's pointed finger to the forested wonders of the Berkshires bordering New York State.

EIGHT

THE QUABBIN RESERVOIR

Drowned in Time

THEY CAME DRESSED IN TUXES AND DRESS SUITS, GOWNS, AND high heels. A grand march opened the evening; a military floor show followed. Then there was the dancing. The orchestra played swing music. The floorboards vibrated.

Children, who weren't allowed to attend, climbed fire escapes to peer in through windows. And others, because the event was sold out, milled around outside the building and the downtown streets.

They were all waiting for one thing, the culmination of this evening: the stroke of midnight. But this wasn't New Year's Eve; it wasn't a Cinderella story. At 12:01 a.m. on April 18, 1938, their towns would officially cease to exist. Water from the dammed up Swift River, once a lifeblood of their valley, would soon creep over the land that they and their ancestors had known for so long. The locations of their family farms, main streets, churches, general stores, community halls, town greens, mills, railroad stations, the very building in which they now gathered, even their hallowed burial grounds—all would be swallowed by the achingly slow rising waters filling up the mighty Quabbin Reservoir. Already, as former residents gathered in the Enfield Town Hall to mark the waning hours at this "Farewell Party and Ball," much of the area around them had been stripped clean. But by the end, anything structural, any vestige of greenery, would be torn down or burned, reduced to a barren, lifeless surface akin to a desert or the surface of the moon.

It was the perilous sliver of time at the twilight of the Great Depression as World War II was brewing in Europe. And in central Massachusetts, it was all the more somber and uncertain. The towns of Enfield, Dana, Greenwich, and Prescott—and slices of surrounding others—were to be inundated with water, their roughly 2,500 residents displaced in one of the largest public works projects in the history of New England.

Man-made reservoir and damming projects have been a frequent occurrence throughout history, an indicator of the march of progress and civilization. In more recent history, they have required the sacrifice of some for the greater benefit of many. And although town washouts and resident relocation has occurred elsewhere across the country—including more locally in Maine and Rhode Island—the building of the Quabbin and the lost towns it claimed has commanded particular attention due to both its human story and its grand scale.

When viewed on a map today, the reservoir appears as an uneven squiggle of a "W"—a charted example of humankind's physical mark on the land and our efforts to reroute and shift water to our will. The centerpiece of a protected watershed that is both an "accidental wilderness" and modern-day recreational treasure, the Quabbin holds 412 billion gallons of water when full. This supplies 140 million gallons daily to roughly 40 percent of the Massachusetts population.

And nearly a century after its building, it continues to be a modern engineering marvel: It is one of the largest unfiltered water sources in the United States, among the biggest dams in the eastern part of the country, its aqueduct one of the longest in the world.

Its building was both celebrated and controversial, its multifaceted story one of loss, gain, renewal—the few who had to give up everything so that others could ensure that, when they turned on their taps, the most essential life source would come flowing out.

DEEP HISTORY

As was the case throughout the northeast prior to the arrival of European settlers, natives frequented the Swift River Valley centuries before it bore its English name. Specifically, the Nipmuc tribe lived in the area and fished the sluiceway's fertile depths. "Quabbin" was what they called it then; the word loosely translates to "the meeting place of many waters," or "a well-watered place." Little could the natives know how morbidly apt that name would be hundreds of years past their inhabitation. But then again, they were exiled first—not by water, but by waves of colonists.

Those settlers began arriving in the 1730s, establishing farming communities throughout the valley. They prided themselves on their independence, illustrating this early on with their participation in Shays' Rebellion, a series of violent attacks on courthouses and other government buildings in Massachusetts in 1786 and 1787. The armed uprising throughout the western and central part of the state was sparked by Daniel Shays and fellow ex-Revolutionary War soldiers who opposed state efforts to collect taxes amidst a post-war debt crisis. Hard-fought but squelched, the insurrection ultimately contributed to the debate over the framing of the new U.S. Constitution.

The area continued to grow and thrive throughout the 1800s, with factories, mills, and farming supporting residents. The four ill-fated towns were established in the early part of the century:

Greenwich (pronounced phonetically) in 1800; Dana in 1801; Enfield in 1816; and Prescott in 1822.

Sandwiched between the three other towns and sharing borders with all, Greenwich had grist mills and factories that manufactured buttons, brooms, hats, and sleighs. Locals also harvested cranberries in bogs on town outskirts. There was even a golf course and a stone clubhouse on a 163-acre farm (completed just a year before the valley was officially condemned). And at the town's celebrated annual "Old Home Days," townspeople gathered for music, dance, and food.

Dana, the northeastern most of the towns, was a similarly lively community; its assortment of mills, taverns, homes, four Protestant congregations, and Roman Catholic church clustered around its classic New England common (one of the sparse vestiges of the former townships that can still be visited today). The mines within its borders yielded potash and soapstone, and rye was an important crop. Logging was a strong economic force, as were its factories that manufactured boxes, table legs, hats, and pocketbooks.

By contrast, Enfield, to the southwest, was hilly and pastorally scenic; its Quabbin Hill offered sweeping views of the entire valley below. Townspeople were principally farmers, although additional income came from ice harvesting. Most of the thousands of tons of ice culled required a communal effort, and the frozen gains of that bounty were sorted and shared among locals.

Finally, Prescott, capping the northwest corner of the quartet of villages, was a religiously diverse community of Congregationalists, Baptists, Presbyterians, and Methodists. It was named for Colonel William Prescott, who commanded the Battle of Bunker Hill in Boston during the first British Siege of the Revolutionary War. Situated on hilly terrain, it was the most rural and least populated of the four towns. Wealthy residents summered there, while locals tended dairy farms, plum orchards, vineyards, and a charcoal kiln. They also hunted pheasants and deer that were shipped to New York City restaurants.

But as the years progressed, cities and towns further out became more populous and prosperous, and local industry and agriculture suffered with the arrival of mass-produced goods brought in by major railroads. These bypassed the area, as did electricity lines. The Swift River Valley became all the more isolated—this exacerbated by residents uprooting themselves to pursue more fruitful opportunities elsewhere. In retrospect, it seems as though they made the right choice.

A PRISTINE SOURCE

The state capital of Boston, by contrast, was a booming metropolis: It was establishing its reputation as "The Hub" with its burgeoning academic, cultural, art, and economic assets. But its rapid population growth and development was straining water supplies, which were little more than a miscellany of unhealthy, poorly filtered systems—including from the long-polluted Charles River. In the early-to-mid 1800s, in fact, drinking and washing water heavily contaminated by sewage or industry led to typhoid fever epidemics. With limited resources in the Boston metropolitan area, state officials began looking elsewhere. Boston was simply too big, too important, to the state's identity and economy to not have a steady, suitable source of water.

Groundwater and surrounding rivers were explored first but were deemed inadequate. So, the state looked further west. In 1848, the Massachusetts General Court authorized the construction of the Cochituate Aqueduct to bring water in from its namesake lake spanning the borders of Wayland and Natick. That effort merely moved back a few homes. Thirty years later, with Cochituate water levels growing perilously low, the state built an aqueduct and five new reservoirs on the Sudbury River in Framingham. But soon enough, that source also became overburdened.

Officials continued going farther and farther west. Unfortunately, procuring a sizable, reliable, clean water supply that would allow the city to continue to prosper would require the suffering and forfeiture of others. The state proved it was willing to impose its will in this regard when, at the turn of the century, it constructed the Wachusett Reservoir at the joining point of the Stillwater, Nashua, and Quinapoxet rivers. This involved the flooding of roughly a half-dozen square miles across West Boylston, Boylston, Clinton, and Sterling. More than 1,700 residents were displaced.

Still, it simply wasn't enough.

As early as 1895, even before the Wachusett Reservoir project was underway, the Swift River Valley caught the attention of politicians and health experts. While continuing full speed with Wachusett, the state sent engineers and surveyors out to scout the Valley and test the Swift River for water purity. Little did the area's insular, homesteading residents know that, even then, their fates were all but determined.

When the Wachusett Reservoir did, indeed, prove deficient almost as soon as it filled to capacity in 1908, Commonwealth officials determined that the Swift River Valley would be next—and on a much more massive scale. It was an ideal choice: The area had a large, clean, high source of water with a modest population around it. Three branches of the Swift River and a tributary of the Connecticut River flowed through its basin, and the hills surrounding it served as natural barriers. A Metropolitan District Water Supply Commission was formed in 1919 to head the project, and they reported: "The valley was the location for a reservoir, not only due to its geography and topography, but also the declining rural nature of the towns, the low density of their population, (and) the lack of any major cultural or economic landmarks."

The commission held their ensuing meetings in Boston. What had previously been a whispered rumor about towns being flooded was indeed becoming realized—but Valley residents had little say in the matter. They could only sit back helplessly as news funneled in. Massachusetts did face a lawsuit from the state of Connecticut claiming that waters rightfully meant to flow into the Connecticut River were being illegally diverted. Connecticut lost.

As one local, Warren Doubleday, told Thomas Conuel for his book *Quabbin: The Accidental Wilderness*: "It was three-thousand people arguing with two million people. We didn't stand much of a chance." It was troubling and heartbreaking to think that drinking water for affluent strangers in Boston was more important than the homes they had made and the ancestral roots they had put down.

The commission developed plans as swift as the river itself, initially pitching them to the state in 1921. Several delays and reevaluations followed, with newspapers across the region early on seizing on the story. One November 1920 headline from *The Boston Globe* proclaimed: "Towns Facing Devastating Flood Because Boston Must Have Water."

But the state persisted in its efforts. In 1927, the decision became final: The Massachusetts legislature approved the Swift River Act, which ordered disincorporation of Dana, Enfield, Greenwich, and Prescott. This also granted the authority and the funding to take property in the area by eminent domain.

Residents, who were never given a voice or a choice and whose destinies were predetermined by a monolithic entity more than eighty miles away, were shocked and stunned. Their homes, their farms, the birthplace of their ancestors—all would soon be drowned.

A DAMNABLE UNDERTAKING

Almost immediately after the Act passed, the outsiders descended, heralding destruction.

In a further unique twist to an already unprecedented story, hundreds of workers, engineers, sanitation and soil experts, geologists and others essentially moved into an area they had been tasked with destroying. Literally. They rented local houses, shopped at area businesses, attended town churches. Becoming embedded in the communities as they did their work, some even joined sports teams and local bands, became chummy with residents, even dated—and in some cases, eventually married—local women.

It was considered a "community of necessity." With the country in the throes of the Great Depression, they couldn't afford to go elsewhere. Employment was as precious as the water they were working to dam up. The project provided somewhere between 3,000 and 5,000 much-needed jobs, some of these even to local residents, too. They so desperately needed work that they had no other choice but to aid in their community's demise.

The mingled assortment of workers soon set to their monumental, grueling—and for some, no doubt soul-crushing—task. A diversion tunnel was constructed first to redirect the mighty Swift River from its bed and allow for the construction of the Winsor Dam and Goodnough Dike at opposite ends of the intended reservoir. The building of both commenced in the mid-1930s. The massive earth-filled dam, named for its chief engineer Frank E. Winsor, would eventually stand a commanding 170 feet above the riverbed and span 2,640 feet in length. The dike opposite, named for its chief engineer Xanthus Henry Goodnough, consisted of watertight chambers buried beneath millions of pounds of earth. It would extend more than 2,000 feet.

To pipe the reservoir's water east also required the creation of a 27-mile underground aqueduct. The tunnel had to be blasted, then sealed with concrete. It was considered the most dangerous part of the project. And indeed, construction of the reservoir claimed the lives of twenty-six men—more than half of those during the building of the aqueduct.

Still, despite its historic implications, little remains of the project's daily ins and outs. Most of the records pertaining to the Quabbin's building were lost when two Metropolitan Water District Commission buildings caught fire in 1939. These included numerous files, water samples, engineering equipment, and engineers' personal property. It was fire and water, it seems, literally warring.

A BARREN LAND

Concurrently with the dam, dike, and aqueduct construction, workers began unceremoniously clearing the valley to its bare soil. For the water to be purely suitable for drinking water, it had to be completely stripped. Men nicknamed "woodpeckers"—dubbed as such by locals due to their perceived inexperience—were paid 62.5 cents an hour for their part in this immense undertaking.

Some families who received compensation under eminent domain—an average of $108 per acre—began their exodus, either leaving their longtime homes empty or having them dismantled and rebuilt in outlying towns. One family, the Thayers, even had their small, boxy, two-story colonial loaded onto a makeshift trailer and towed away by a Model T. "The houses were going down and everybody was moving out," Sally Norcross, a former resident of Dana, recalled in an interview years after the dreadful fact. "It was going to be a dead town, that's all we knew."

Sixteen miles of tracks for the local "Rabbit Road"—which ran through the valley as it connected Athol and Enfield—were ripped up. Eight train stations were razed. Monuments to fallen Civil War soldiers were felled themselves and moved elsewhere. Prescott's Congregational Church was one of the few salvaged structures; it was transferred piece by piece to South Hadley, where it now serves as a museum. Whatever standing structures that remained—mills, stores, houses—were demolished and bulldozed to their foundations and empty cellar holes. Their contents were sold or auctioned off. Trees were hacked down, their stumps dislodged; brush was lopped; topsoil scraped clear. The land was effectively scoured and burned.

Some say the valley was alit for months—throughout the day and deep into the night—the once clean country air clogged with smoke.

Don McMillan, a resident of nearby Hardwick, recalled what it was like to watch all this from afar. "We would sit on the porch of our house, and the western sky was aglow at night from the flames of the burning brush in the valley," he told author Michael Tougias. "It was eerie."

One particularly startling image captured a Civil War statue standing in silhouette against a wall of flame engulfing the steeple of the Enfield church. Another shows the Enfield town office once stripped of that status—a lone stone building standing in the center of a ravaged landscape, its windows cleared of glass staring out like vacant eyes. Photographers also captured workers in overalls and newsie's hats posing on the partially completed dam, leading debris-filled horse carts, or standing with their implements in leveled fields.

Also, as part of the project, more than 7,600 bodies were exhumed from the valley's nearly three dozen cemeteries—an act that was all at once reverential and self-serving. Should they be left in place, the graves would be doubly buried under hundreds of feet of water, with loved ones never able to visit them again. At the same time, it was unacceptable to have human remains at the bottom of the reservoir; they could contaminate the water supply. Family members, in some cases several generations removed, were contacted; they were given the option of having family members reinterred at a cemetery of their choosing or at the newly established Quabbin Park Cemetery in Ware. This pastoral graveyard was established at the southernmost part of the watershed and was specifically intended for the valley's twice-buried dead.

As part of the process, every grave was photographed in its original location, headstones were carefully recorded, and new pine boxes were provided for remains, however scant they were. Once graves were dug up, a designated hearse conveyed the dead to their new places of rest. This was all overseen by Clifton Moore, an undertaker and native of Enfield. The state covered all costs of transportation and reburial. But not all were accounted for; some disintegrating tombstones were found underwater during a scuba dive in the late 1990s. Similarly, the burial grounds of local tribal members remained unmarked, now left forever to obscurity under gallons of fresh water.

Not surprisingly, many residents considered the digging up of their family members—and the disruption of their eternal rest—just another insult, and a morbid and sacrilegious one at that. Lois Barnes of Prescott remembered her mother, one of the last governing officials of the town, staying up late into the night to lend her signature to permits for gravesite relocation.

"The next day, on the way to school, I'd be seeing them digging up the bones," she marveled to a *Hartford Courant* reporter years later. "Isn't that a strange thing?"

Finally, in 1939, when every last remnant of human habitation and vegetation were scrubbed, the diversion tunnel was removed and the Swift River was unleashed. As it resumed its natural flow, the waters of the new reservoir slowly rose behind the dam and dike. The reservoir took seven years to fill to full capacity of 412 billion gallons—what might be considered a slow, torturous death by drowning.

Side-by-side photos taken from overlooking ridges illustrated the progression of the project: first a verdant valley clustered with boxy buildings and church steeples; then the area stripped clean to its foothills, the only evidence of human life the curvy tracings of abandoned roads; and finally filled with water, hills that once loomed over the towns transformed to mere islands.

The Quabbin Reservoir was full, for the first time, in June 1946—and all that had once thrived in the valley was swallowed by 150 feet of water.

MEMORIES AFLOAT

Before their submersion, the four towns had a combined population of roughly 2,500, many of these fourth and fifth generation families. Their communities consisted of dozens of homes and sixty summer camps, more than a half-dozen churches serving several faiths, a dozen schools, and numerous mills, stores, taverns, hotels, town buildings, and recreation areas.

Their ousting left people scattered; some of the more sheltered residents had never even ventured beyond the valley and barely knew where to begin to cultivate new roots. They fanned out throughout surrounding towns, even as the money they received through eminent domain was barely adequate to establish new homes, farms, and businesses.

Much like the aftermath of death, many former residents could never fully process the loss or reconcile the sacrifice—they were doomed for life to continue looking backward. All they had left were memories; the old adage was doubly true for them: They could never go home again.

"That was the only place we'd ever known," now-deceased Bob Wilder, an Enfield native and local historian, told reporters in an interview decades later. "I try not to get mad when I think about it anymore, but that was home."

His family had settled in the area before the Revolutionary War, and he remembered riding away from his hometown in a family friend's ice-hauling truck loaded with a few possessions and farm animals. Just a schoolboy at the time, he was accompanied by his parents, grandparents, and siblings. The bodies of thirteen of his ancestors had already been relocated to new burial grounds.

It was only natural that people were bitter, he noted. "You'd be bitter if you saw our little town, and they took it away from you—'they' being this organization out in Boston. We didn't know them."

Richard Rohan, another former Enfield resident, echoed this sentiment, conveying to reporters how upsetting the exile was for his family. "They did not care too much for the people of Boston, let's put it that way," he said.

Although the scars ran too deep for many families to ever want to broach the issue again, those who did lamented the fact that locals were paid for their houses as pure brick-and-mortar (as it were) structures—not their homes, their livelihoods, their community statuses. Former community leaders, matriarchs and patriarchs blended into the general citizenry. Neighbors, friends, and classmates were separated by miles instead of a few houses or blocks.

They recalled the simple things that formed a community: "Old Home Days" celebrations, sledding on Quabbin Hill, blueberry picking, canoeing and fishing the area's numerous lakes and ponds, picnics, balls, church festivals, town anniversary celebrations, cooking parties where women applied their homegrown recipes with "a pinch of this" or "a tip of the jug of molasses." And pre-flood pictures depict simple, everyday life: Well-dressed men lounging in front of the combination country store and post office; children playing hide and seek; families posing in front of their modest clapboard homes; boys gathering up hay with makeshift land rakes.

Many also described the bittersweet gala on Wednesday April 27, 1938, that brought them all together one last time. Sponsored by the Enfield Fire Department, it was a commemoration of "the passing of the Town of Enfield and Swift River Valley," according to its promotional poster. Tickets were $1 for the dance, 50 cents for the concert, with "dress informal" (although considering the occasion, its attendees did quite the opposite). Drawing more than 1,000 people and covered heavily by regional press, the catered event started out with a grand march, and featured a half-hour floor show from Billy Syner's Unit No. 1 and a concert with a ten-piece set by McEnelly's Orchestra. Dancing was held from 9 a.m. to 2 p.m., with "lunch at midnight." As the poster proclaimed: "Come old timers, newcomers and friends of all for a last good time, whether you dance or not."

Still, not all memories were rosy. One unnamed former resident interviewed by the *Historical Journal of Massachusetts* described his hometown of Prescott as a "dead and dying" place. There were no educational or economic opportunities for young people, and "the quicker you got out the better." "The Quabbin was the best thing to happen to the Valley," he told his interviewers.

Others have conceded that, had the towns not been flooded, their rural, agrarian character would have instead been washed away by the ongoing procession of progress—subdivisions, highways, strip malls. What makes the Quabbin story all the more interesting is the fact that it locked these lost towns effectively in their own time capsule.

And many have worked tirelessly to ensure that, even if the communities are physically gone, they are not forgotten. The Swift River Valley Historical Society is the foremost source of artifacts, having catalogued and scanned thousands of photos, and recorded and digitized dozens of interviews with former residents. The Quabbin story and its societal, cultural, and historical implications has continued to fascinate: It has been the subject of countless newspaper accounts, archival projects, thesis papers, books both nonfiction and fiction alike, written and oral histories, documentaries, discussions, tours, and exploratory scuba dives.

What's more, a Friends of Quabbin volunteer group once held regular events including Tuesday Teas that welcomed reminiscing locals; commemorative balls over the decades also marked somber anniversaries. In a sense, the Valley's untimely demise caused it to be ever more well documented and celebrated than it likely might have been had it been allowed to survive.

But now more than eighty years removed from the events, few, if any, survivors remain. As former residents grew to old age, though, they always remembered their towns—and their hope was that time would, too.

A RENEWED PURPOSE

If you're in central Massachusetts and it's a nice day for a walk, you're more likely than not to hear: "Let's go out to the Quabbin."

Today, the watershed around the reservoir is referred to as an "accidental wilderness" and wildlife refuge—and it is also a vast, cherished, recreational treasure. The manmade water body sits at the center of a protected watershed comprising 120,000 acres sprawled across 39 square miles. The majority of this is owned by the Massachusetts Department of Conservation and Recreation; the remainder is permanently protected by state agencies and organizations including *Massachusetts Wildlife*, *Mass Audubon*, the Trustees of Reservations, and Harvard Forest. This unique forest hydrology efficiently holds back sediment and other undesirable elements, making the reservoir's water remarkably clean.

The area is traced with hundreds of miles of trails for hiking and biking; particularly around the reservoir proper, the starting point for most of these are numbered gates. Paths bring visitors through forests and across fields to various spots along the water's edge with beaches of speckled and smoothed rocks. A walk along the roughly half-mile-long Winsor Dam offers 180-degree views of the reservoir and the landscape extending far beyond. A colossal structure with precipitous drop-offs to land on one side and water on the other, it is a tangible reminder of all that went into building this place.

One of the only high and dry remnants of the underwater ghost towns is the former site of Dana Common. It can be accessed via Gate 40 off Route 32A in rural Petersham and requires a roughly two-mile trek down a gravel road through the woods. The spot is little more than a rough oval patch of grass encircled by the ruins of cellar holes. Stone markers announce the site's designation on the National Register of Historic Places as well as its dedication to "all those who sacrificed their homes and ways of life." Small placards indicate the structures that the cellar holes once supported: Dana's Cotton General Store, a church, a school, and residences, including that of the Johnson family.

Otherwise, though, few vestiges remain—those walking the expansive trail system throughout the watershed might unexpectedly come upon sparse, grown over, crumbling and collapsing stone walls and cellar holes; the occasional set of stone steps leading to nowhere; rusted, unintelligible remnants of rusted metal; stubborn trees that have grown up around impeding debris (such as narrow saplings pushing themselves up between the narrow slats of an old metal bed headboard).

Visitors can also tour the Quabbin Park Cemetery or drive the road that curves its way around the huge body of water and offers the occasional turn-off offering scenic views. It is, without a doubt, a beautiful, tranquil spot. But gazing out over the water, it's difficult not to remember its much deeper history, and the deteriorating remains of the once lively towns buried far beneath its watery depths. The final truth is that these ghost towns were not forsaken; they were drowned.

NINE

THE CAPE

Isolated Experiences

ONE OF CAPE COD'S MOST DISTINCTIVE TRAITS IS ITS SHAPE: IT juts out into the Atlantic from the Massachusetts mainland, a flexed arm with a balled fist. Hollowed and carved for millennia by the ocean and the elements and their ceaseless cycle of destruction and creation, its exposed protuberance is characteristic and instantly recognizable.

Named in 1602 by explorer Bartholomew Gosnold—and that, fittingly, for its plentiful codfish population—the hooked peninsula today deals in tourism as it once did in fishing and maritime trades. It attracts visitors from around the world with its picturesque white sandy beaches, historic lighthouses, snug harbors, oyster flats, fishing communities, seashores cluttered with quaintly weathered cottages, abundant recreational opportunities, and hipstery hubs of arts and culture.

And it is, in a sense, an on-and-off ghost town all its own—its borders ebbing and flowing as dramatically as the tides with the whims of tourists. In summer months, it is a riot of life, and the two main thoroughfares leading into it are notoriously gridlocked for miles on end. In the winter, by stark contrast—particularly in its farthest nooks, inlets, and harbors—it is all but abandoned with the mass exodus of visitors and so-called snowbirds.

But there are former towns and villages here that remain deserted to the ages. Once vibrant communities brimming with life and industry, their hardworking residents were driven away by decreased opportunities, the cruel and unforgiving fancies of Mother Nature, and the desperate burden of isolation.

WHITEWASH VILLAGE

Located on Monomoy Island, an eight-mile-long spit of land extending into the sea from Cape Cod's elbow, Whitewash Village was for but thirty years a thriving seaside community. The area's title as an "island" is only accurate half of the time: When the warring factions of the Atlantic (to the east) and Nantucket Sound (to the west) clash, they cause dangerous "rips" over shallow shoals and bars and often engulf and isolate the furthest sections of the narrow, ribbony point. Due to this perilous location—a battleground against the forces of water, wind, and the ever-lenient sand caught between the two—the village seemed doomed from the start.

But long before that, for several centuries before European arrival, a local tribe known as the Monomoiyicks used the area as a summer base for shell fishing and hunting. Later, it became a cattle feeding ground for colonists living closer to the mainland. Whitewash had simple beginnings in the way of "Stewarts Tavern," which opened in 1711. Eventually, drawn by the bounty of the sea, settlers began trickling in and building simple houses around the popular sailor watering hole.

The village is believed to have taken its name from the whitewashed cliffs and rocks surrounding it. These could still be seen in 1864, just a few years after the town's demise. From a descriptive, epic poem-like article that year in *Harper's Monthly*: "On its prominent edifices, there was, in some former era, bestowed a coating of that economical pigment, remains of which can even now be detected by a careful observation of these outer walls." That same piece referred to Monomoy as a "strip of sand averaging little more than a quarter of a mile in width—in shape a miniature Cape Cod."

Today, the area is a locale of several names, including Sandy Point and Powder Hole Harbor. Monomoy, in turn, gave its name to a lightweight, crudely constructed, utilitarian whaleboat that was rowed or sailed under all conditions for use in general ship work or to pursue whales.

The area's roiling waters and unforgiving winds earned Monomoy a direful reputation almost as soon as boats began sailing the sea. It came to be known as "Cape Mallebarre," an ancient French term translating to "Cape of Evil Bars"—and soon thereafter, the "graveyard of the Atlantic." Shipwrecks off Monomoy were a frequent occurrence, with even the most experienced sailors discombobulated by the ever-shifting seas and sand.

With the rapid growth in post-Revolutionary War marine traffic, lightships (oil lamps mounted on tall masts) were erected around the shoals. By 1823, the U.S. government finally acted, approving roughly $3,000 for a lighthouse on Monomoy Point. Consisting of a brick keeper's dwelling with a wooden tower and iron lantern room atop it, it was Cape Cod's fifth light tower at the time.

Whitewash was built about a mile from the lighthouse, and at its most populous had a population of two hundred. The village consisted of a school (Public School #13, so it was identified) for roughly a dozen students, as well as cottages, numerous storage sheds, a lodging house, hotel, and the Monomoy, or Monomoit House. *Harper's* 1864 account called the latter a "weather-beaten, barracky, amphibious structure, fishermen and coasters' fitting-store on the first floor, lodging-house and excursionists' inn on the second, besides the fitting-out store of __ & Co., and a motley array of storage and packing sheds perfumed with fish-oil." The "amphibious" description was an apt one: During certain high tides, the sea came partway up its front stairs, and patrons had to visit it by boat.

A black-and-white illustration from the magazine depicts a harbor clustered with several slope-roofed houses and what looks to be a tavern. A masted ship is moored at the docks, and in the foreground a man pulls a dinghy out of the water onto a sand and beach grass-covered mound.

As would be expected for the location, residents relied solely on the ocean, making a living catching cod and mackerel in the natural deep harbor; this was then dried and packed for sale at markets in Boston and New York City. They also caught lobster—today a cherished, pricey indulgence but then considered a lower-class food—that they sold to mainlanders for two cents a pound. Clamming and duck hunting were integral to village life.

Then there were those known as "wreckers," who also relied on the sea—or humans' attempted dominion of it. They persisted on steady shipwrecks, either rowing out to stranded and abandoned boats or waiting as they were churned to shore with a rising surge. Lookouts, or "pointers" were even assigned. As *Harper's* described it: "And when sounds the warning cry, 'Wreck, oh!' what a scampering there is among the Pointers!" And if "fates were propitious," cotton and flour would be removed, along with topmasts, yards, and running rigging, "and the stout ship is steadily stripped."

And that down to the skeletons of its hull: The winter fires of Monomoy were described as burning "with strange hues from black wreck-wood seasoned in many climes." Family wood piles consisted of many a frame bound with jointings, bolts, spokes, and treenails, "torn apart by crow-bar and levers of curious design, and beetle and wedge, and pick and axe."

Daily life was dictated by the sea, with children even dismissed from school at the call of "Whale-Ho!" to help harvest blubber from beached whales.

But by the 1860s, the fury of the Atlantic and the unforgiving weather proved too much for human habitation. A hurricane caused the harbor to shoal over; fish stocks were also on the decrease. Islanders moved to stabler areas of the Cape or the mainland; some of them were said to have dismantled their homes, "taking with them even roof-tree and hearth-stone," as described by *Harper's*. A few of these are believed to have been rebuilt in Chatham at the very tip of the Cape before its arm extends sharply north.

"The golden age of Monomoy has passed away," the maudlin *Harper's* decried. "There is a shadow of sadness on the glory of Monomoy."

Still the angry ocean needed monitoring for the sake of mariners. Monomoy's Life Saving Station was established in 1872, working in tandem with the lighthouse. Keepers continued to tend the light station—living on Monomoy year-round with their families—until it was decommissioned in 1923 and replaced by the more powerful Chatham Light. The U.S. Coast Guard stayed on until 1945, monitoring for rumrunners during Prohibition, then German U-boats during World War II. The island did earn scars in World War II: Archaeologists have since found bullets lodged in the lighthouse, allegedly from target practice.

The Monomoy National Wildlife Refuge was established in 1944 to provide habitat for migratory birds. The U.S. Government officially gave the island a "wilderness" status under the 1964 Wilderness Act, which sought to protect 9.1 million acres of federal lands. Today, it is under the care of the U.S. Fish and Wildlife Service and serves as a refuge for several threatened and endangered bird species, including the piping plover, American oystercatcher, roseate tern, and red knot, as well as the endangered northeastern beach tiger beetle, and the threatened plant—the seabeach amaranth. It is also home to dozens of other species of birds such as egrets, herons, petrels, and grebes, and contains the United State's largest grey seal haul-out (the pinniped version of lounging around). The refuge is traced with a trail system, as well, and welcomes passive recreation.

Monomoy continues to be half-island, half-peninsula, depending on the will of the tides and wind. Its solitary sentinel continues its ceaseless watch: The bright red lighthouse stands tall over the dunes, accompanied by the former keeper's house with its weathered shingles and boarded-up windows. Some have compared it to a "minaret in the Sahara," referencing the towers that jut out congruously from that African desert.

It is a final vestige of the brief period when humans attempted to conquer this beleaguered claw of land—which ultimately won out.

LONG POINT

Located at the extreme tip of Cape Cod as the arm of land begins curling back into itself, Long Point may as well be an island all its own. An isolated finger pointing back at the peninsula, it is surrounded by water in all directions: the Atlantic and Massachusetts Bay to the north and northwest, Cape Cod Bay to the southwest, Provincetown Harbor to the southeast, and East Harbor and salt marsh to the east. A rock jetty is the only physical connection to the rest of the land—and all that effectively keeps it from being a true island. The lighthouse sitting on its very precipice is one of the furthermost, and thus most remote, spots on the entire Cape.

All this ultimately makes the area exposed, unsettled, dangerous, even deadly. Long Point's curvature is a natural barrier for Provincetown and its harbor, meaning it takes the brunt force and battering of wind and sea. "This sickle of sand which encloses one of the finest harbors on the North Atlantic was so narrow that encroaching storms played havoc with it and threatened at one time to sweep the narrow point away," Mary Heaton Vorse wrote in her 1942 book, *Time and the Town: A Provincetown Chronicle.*

Still, for centuries, it has attracted humans with its bounteous sea life and beautiful scenery. The Wampanoag and Nauset tribes were likely the first to frequent the area around 3,000 to 2,000 BCE. As legend has it, the famous Vikings Leif Erikson and his brother Thorwald also stopped by during their extensive explorations of the uncharted world; as, it is believed, did fishermen from Basque (a southwestern European ethnic group) as they followed cod routes.

Because of the fertile fishing waters surrounding it, Long Point became a natural choice for a fishing settlement. John Atwood built the first house on the jutting spot of land in 1818. Just four years later, the first baby was born on the Point: Prince Freeman, Jr. Others continued to follow, attracted by the opportunity for abundant mackerel, shad, and bass hauls. And it proved prosperous: There were reports that seventy-five, 200-pound barrels of white shad could be caught in one haul using handcrafted seines, or large nets. Barrels could fetch $16 apiece.

The point's other profitable enterprise: salt harvesting. The Atlantic naturally provided an endless supply, and the process was low cost. Windmills pumped seawater into saltwork drying pans. The salt supported the local fishing industry, which used it in preserving fish for shipment. Long Point's saltworks had an annual output of between 280,000 and 335,000 pounds—or "five to six hundred hogsheads"—of "extra quality salt."

Increasing boat traffic—and ensuing shipwrecks—around the Point and Provincetown demanded the need for a lighthouse, which was erected in 1827 for a cost of $2,500. Just three years later, it hosted the Point's first school, which started out with just three pupils. By 1846, the area was home to thirty-eight fishing families with roughly 200 adults and sixty children, and growth prompted the building of a dedicated schoolhouse. By the mid-1800s, there was also a post office, general store, a wharf and boat landings for twenty vessels, and several saltworks with eight windmills that pumped seawater into roughly 8,000 feet of drying pans. An existing stereoscopic image depicts one of the squat structures with its rectangular wooden blades flanked by a man and a horse, overlooking sloping fields and fences.

Writer Josef Berger later described the convivial atmosphere of the time in the *Cape Cod Pilot*: "It was an exciting neighborhood to live in. Children who might have been afraid of dogs elsewhere, here ran from the sharks."

Still, it could be a harsh environment—particularly in the winter when Mother Nature releases her full fury—not to mention a detached, secluded one. There was not one single road leading into or out of Provincetown, let alone Long Point, until the late-1800s. This made land travel by foot the only option: Trekkers had to traverse more than four miles of tall, shifting sand dunes and thin strips of beach. And even this was impossible twice a day during high tide or with storm washouts (unless you were willing to wade, that is). Tempestuous weather mocked early attempts to rectify this: A wooden bridge was built over East Harbor in 1854, only to be destroyed in a winter storm two years later. It was eventually rebuilt, but it was only reliable about half the time due to the area's frequent storms. The railroad didn't reach the Provincetown area until 1873, and the Provincetown Causeway, which provides foot access to this day, wasn't constructed until 1911.

These sporadic, unreliable land routes made Provincetown and Long Point de facto islands: Residents relied on the sea when it came to travel, commerce, communication, and ultimate survival. Procuring everyday needs was problematic, too: Notably, there was no source of fresh water on Long Point, so plank cisterns were built throughout the village to collect rainwater. And if rain was scarce or there was a full-on drought? Barrels were filled in Provincetown and transported along the several-mile land route.

This secluded and primitive way of life, coupled with critical economic factors, caused Long Point's population to sharply decline in the 1850s. For one, salt production became far less lucrative due to local and national competition: By mid-century, Provincetown had seventy-eight saltworks, and completion of the Erie Canal meant for more widespread shipment of salt from deposits in Syracuse, New York. With so much available, the price of the mineral dropped to $1 per bushel from a high of roughly $8 per bushel. Exacerbating that, demand for salt-cured fish was declining as ice harvesting and storage was on the increase.

Meanwhile, Long Point suffered the man-made plight of several other coastal communities in the mid-1800s: Offshore waters were becoming exhausted of their fish stocks due to overharvesting.

Even as locals began their exodus, they didn't want to completely abandon all they had built. They packed up what they could—even their homes. One of the local deacon's specialties was moving buildings, so thirty structures were carefully shimmied onto rafts and dinghies and floated or towed across the harbor to Provincetown. They were then relocated throughout the sister town and many still stand today. These include the former post office, now at 256 Bradford Street, and the schoolhouse, now on Commercial Street. Their unique journeys are commemorated with blue and white plaques.

As Vorse wryly wrote of the undertaking, "They say that so gently were these houses eased off that the moving didn't interfere with the housewife cooking her dinner." Another writer for the *Cape Cod Standard Times* provided this droll description: "Perhaps the inhabitants grew tired of sharks sunning themselves on their front lawns, perhaps sea creatures carried off their pet dogs and cats; whatever the reason the citizens of Long Point scheduled a colossal moving day. . . . And that was the end of the community of Long Point."

By 1861, just two houses and the lighthouse remained on Long Point. But as the Civil War was pitting north against south, the peninsula-off-a-peninsula found new purpose as a military battery. Men were stationed there around the clock at two battery houses with eight combined guns, and one of the remaining homes was repurposed as officer's headquarters. Still, for whatever reason, the Long Point Battery was derided by locals, who mocked it as "Fort Useless" and "Fort Ridiculous." Indeed, it saw no action, and when the war ended in 1865, Long Point was once again deserted.

And then, repurposed once more. A decade later, in 1875, Cape Cod Oil Works began using the Long Point wharf to extract all usable materials from whale and fish carcasses. An old ship hull was even dragged up to the factory and used as a fertilizer screening room. The wharf had been built by first town settler John Atwood. Not much else is known about the company's rise, demise, or much in between, but archives indicate that it was still in operation in 1883. The only existing photograph of it dates to 1891 and depicts its motley assortment of buildings and the recycled hull. Scrawled handwriting on the print tells us that it was "Condemned . . . 2/6/19." The lighthouse also saw a refresh in 1875, when its blunted, octagonal tower was replaced with a square brick structure.

More than a century and a quarter later, even as adjacent Provincetown has grown into an artistic and cultural mecca, Long Point has reverted very nearly to its original pristine state. Only Route

6 traces all the way up the Cape's narrowing forearm to its fist; on a modern map, the driving options diminish right along with the land. And even the road takes visitors almost—but not quite—there: The ocean halts it in Provincetown. Getting out to the point requires a 20-minute ferry ride or a roughly three-mile walk across a rock jetty (the Provincetown Causeway), dunes, and beaches.

The lighthouse, a white squat square topped with a walkway and lantern room, stands alone, incongruously—and to anthropomorphize, you could even say self-consciously—in the middle of the thumb-shaped spit of land. A small outbuilding hunkers a little way away next to a manmade earthen mound from the point's few years as a battery. Atop this: A tall wooden cross has been erected as a memorial to Charles Darby, a Provincetown man killed in World War II.

It is doubly fitting for this ghost town, which has seen all that the tides of time can bring.

TEN

HAYWARDVILLE

Creative Industry

THE CLOSER YOU GET TO BOSTON, THE DENSER THE POPULATION becomes. And with so many people clustered near the state capital, space is a scarce commodity. For this reason, there are few ghost towns to the Massachusetts east—one exception being Haywardville. The small, otherwise unassuming mill town was seemingly like any other that sprang up around water sources throughout New England in the eighteenth and nineteenth centuries—except it boasts a creatively storied past.

Now part of a state reservation, the industrious village was located in Stoneham, a town nine miles north of the Hub. Haywardville's story begins in 1632, when Massachusetts Bay Colony founder John Winthrop discovered Spot Pond Brook. With a rapid and steady flow, the water body would become critical to the hamlet's growth. As early as 1658, land around the brook was being parceled out for woodlots. Then, in 1670, a sawmill and gristmill were built to provide the first settlers with timber and flour.

The village's first contribution to history came during the Revolutionary War: George Washington was said to have used timber from the area to fortify Dorchester Heights. The then-general and his men seized the Heights in March 1776 and expelled the British, thus ending the siege of Boston—the first strategic and political victory for the Continental Army during the Revolutionary War.

When Americans finally won independence after the close of the war, communities grew rapidly around Boston. In Haywardville, seven mills and two mill ponds were soon constructed. These supplied locals with spices, medicines, snuff—and chocolate. In fact, the first reported chocolate factory in the United States is believed to have been located in the village.

Later, a Charles C. "Grampa" Jones took over ownership of the Haywardville mill complex and converted it into an ice storage facility. This coincided with a novel discovery when it came to ice storage: Boston businessman Frederic Tudor (later dubbed "The Ice King") developed a system that limited the rate that ice melted. This involved packing ice as tightly as possible and insulating it with sawdust instead of straw (the longstanding practice). Around the same time, one of his foremen, Nathaniel Wyeth, came up with the practice of dividing frozen bodies of water into chessboard patterns, cutting two-foot-square blocks, and hauling it out with horse-drawn ploughs (previously ice had been laboriously sawn by hand). These new methods enabled a healthy ice trade in Haywardville, Stoneham, and other surrounding towns. Frozen blocks from Spot Pond became a major part of the early ice industry in the nineteenth century; they were shipped all over the United States, and potentially even internationally.

During America's Second Industrial Revolution in the mid-to-late 1800s, factories began taking the place of mills in Haywardville and elsewhere. Silk dyer William Barrett opened the area's first factory, supplementing it with a dye house, living quarters for workers, and a mill pond.

When Barrett died, Elisha Slade Converse purchased the mills and remodeled them for shoe production. The politician, business-man, and philanthropist is best known for founding the Boston Rubber Shoe Company in nearby Malden (where he also served as the first mayor). It was the largest rubber shoe manufacturer in the world at the time. And notably, in 1908, his descendant, Marquis Mills Converse, set his family down in the footwear history books when he established the Converse Rubber Shoe Co. in Malden. This, of course, would become legendary for its popular Converse All-Star basketball shoe—introduced in 1918—and their spinoff "Chuck Taylors," named after the American basketball player who helped to improve and promote them.

Then, in 1858, businessman, inventor, and village namesake Nathaniel Hayward took over the mill complex—ultimately setting the stage for yet another of the town's historical contri-butions. It is believed (at least by some) that Hayward discovered and developed the process of rubber vulcanization, but never got the credit for it. The 1844 patent for the revolutionary method of applying fire and sulfur to render rubber pliable is in the name of his contemporary, the self-taught chemist Charles Goodyear—who would lend his name to the rubber tire company giant. It has been contended, however, that Hayward first discovered the process (and that by accident), while working at a rubber factory in Roxbury, Connecticut. The name "vulcanization" is in reference to Vulcan, the Roman god of fire.

The truth is murky and lost to the ages—but in any case, Hay-wardville Rubber Works produced a variety of rubber products, including boots, fire buckets, spittoons, and apparently also "slick-ers," canvas and rubber raincoats.

At its height, the mill complex powered by water and horse-power consisted of several buildings, as well as a boardinghouse and small shops. But industry began to decline in the second half of the nineteenth century as larger (and ultimately more prosperous) businesses cropped up in the surrounding area. The rapid development of steam and electric power also had a negative impact. One final burst of activity came in the 1880s with F. W. Morandi's mining operations near Spot Pond: He reportedly excavated small quantities of gold and silver.

By the 1890s, the town was but a deserted remnant of its industrious past. The state purchased Haywardville in 1894 and relocated most of its buildings to adjacent Melrose. It is now part of the Middlesex Fells Reservation, a 2,200-acre public recreation area spanning Stoneham, Malden, Medford, and Winchester. Spot sits at its center.

Today, only traces of Haywardville remain in "The Fells," as it is referred to: the remnants of a rectangular brick foundation hemming in land that slowly slopes downward before dead-ending at a brick wall; a narrow brook channel; a squat stone embankment whose entrance has been barred over.

Still, for a small, now long-gone village, Haywardville has left its imprint on history.

ELEVEN

DOGTOWN

A Ruin of Time

IT WAS SAID THAT SHE WAS HIDEOUSLY UGLY; CORPULENT, FRUMPY, possessing two fang-like upper teeth. An old hag with a supposed evil eye and a callous temperament, she made her home—the salacious setting of many fortune-tellings amidst copious drams of rum—in a tumble-down clapboard structure at the entrance to a once-propitious settlement on Gloucester's Cape Ann. The craggy nub protruding into the frigid ocean is about thirty miles northeast of Boston and marks the northern limit of Massachusetts Bay.

Feared and reviled, Tammy Younger was the grand Madame among a motley assortment of supposed soothsayers, witches, outcasts and indigent—those both disdainful of society and spurned by it—who laid claim to a notorious, abandoned north-of-Boston village township known as "Dogtown" that had long been overgrown and forsaken to the elements.

Today, the spot where she once hosted her lewd parties is but a jumble of fallen-down stones taken back by nature; the village where she and her wanton associates practiced their dark arts has devolved and evolved over centuries, now comprising of a bramble of trails traversing forests and fields, swamps and bogs.

Dogtown is a legendary—and some say cautionary—tale of how time can mutate prosperity into negligence. Planned around four roads and originally called the Commons Settlement, the village was established in 1693, according to the Essex National Heritage Area, on a high plateau on Cape Ann as a means of protection from the pirates who trolled the outlying harbor and the Atlantic Ocean. Officials measured out a few dozen lots, several families took up residence, and the area flourished with life and activity.

Still, it wasn't long before contentions arose. As Gloucester shifted from agrarianism, growing comparably along with its flourishing shipbuilding and fishing trades, residents began to talk of splitting off from the Commons Settlement and establishing separate parishes. Then, as the Revolutionary War began to broil and the state legislature sanctioned pirating along the east coast, more and more Gloucester men shipped off to sea (with many never to experience their long-awaited homecoming). Over the next eight years, as was the case throughout the thirteen colonies, the war was decimating. By the time of the signing of the Treaty of Paris in 1783, Gloucester had lost more than 1,000 residents, or nearly one-fifth of its population, according to Elyssa East, author of *Dogtown: Death and Enchantment in a New England Ghost Town.*

Although many areas eventually recovered, the Commons village, due largely to its high, out-of-the-way location—ultimately the prime attraction for its initial siting and settlement—did not. Most of its homes were simply emptied and left to deteriorate as their owners sought more fortuitous work in Gloucester proper and elsewhere.

THE MEEK SHALL INHERIT

With their exodus, the area soon became ramshackle and unkempt, its once well-cared-for homes and pathways reclaimed by its lush environs: Ivy and weeds clamoring about its structures, encroaching trees above its once-wide paths and underbrush below transfiguring them into verdant, narrow tunnels.

This uncultivated and overgrown nature served as a welcoming cloak for the area's destitute and undesirables. Soldiers' widows left impoverished by the war, hobos, drifters, the infirm, and old crones such as Tammy Younger who flouted their sorceress reputations, migrated up to the largely deserted settlement and squatted in the crumbling dwellings of their choosing. The area was also an asylum of sorts for former and runaway slaves and other misbegotten wanderers

Soon the nickname "Dogtown" began to circulate, at first haltingly hushed and whispered, then more hastily slung as a pejorative. According to legend, it originated out of a practice that some considered detrimental for protection: As transients began to encroach, original Commons settlers, many of them widows who couldn't afford to make the exodus south to more desirable areas, started keeping large guard dogs for protection. Over time, as those village foremothers passed, it was said that their canines became homeless, feral and ran wild throughout the area as it became increasingly more neglected.

However, as East explained, the name was ultimately a common, catch-all derogatory term for such disowned locales left to ruin. During the 1800s and early 1900s, there were about sixty different locations, emptied by society's betters and taken over by the downtrodden, with the charged label of "Dogtown" across the United States, Cape Ann's version came to be known for its gypsy nature, as well as the perversities, backward and wayward practices that went unbridled within its limits. Its migratory inhabitants made their meager livings through small-scale farming, berry-picking, and, most infamously, by engaging in prostitution, reading fortunes, and purportedly casting spells. With the area abundant with a literal pharmacy of native herbs and plants, Dog-towners were also said to concoct numerous mystical tonics and potions sought out for their augmentative, healing, intoxicating and aphrodisiacal qualities.

Meanwhile, in gender-bending social-mores-flouting prac-tices, women dressed as men and vice versa, with men performing housework and other so-called feminine chores such as washing and nursing, and their female companions taking up such duties as hauling wood and building stone walls. Such forsaken places also tend to breed fantastical accounts. The supposed conjurers and enchanters who swarmed the area were said to be seen bewitchingly traversing the sky on brooms, including the brazen "Old Meg." Younger, for her part, hosted many card games and fortune-telling parties flowing with rum and revelry. With her arresting evil eye, it was also said she commanded merchants to provide her with what-ever goods she desired. Living at the perimeter of the settlement beside a bridge over a warbling brook, she allegedly flung open the windows of her decrepit abode to squawk obscenities and curses at oxcart drivers daring to attempt passage into or around Dogtown. Should they refuse to leave a token toll of goods or food, the har-ridan would hex their carts—holding their stunned oxen in place, or simply levitating the cargo she desired right out of their wagons before releasing the terrified drivers from their paralysis and allow-ing them to speed off.

Even upon her death at age seventy-six, the dreadful old shrew continued to menace. Her casket-maker abhorred having her presence in his home, his family refusing to sleep with her coffin in their midst. To finally rid themselves of her earthly body and placate her stormy spirit, members of the surrounding community combined funds to pay for a silver-plated coffin.

By night, various pirates, sea captains—as well as local men eager for debauchery—ventured within the elastic and slowly expanding borders of the forgotten village to sip on the women's odd brews, hear about their possible futures, and engage in lascivious acts in its "red light" district. Some of its more well-off and unsuspecting Johns, it was said, simply disappeared and were never heard from again (another method by which the freeloading Dogtowners scrounged for money and goods?). As both time and the vitality of its derelict residents began to wane, Dogtown's population dwindled, then completely petered out. By 1814, just a half-dozen of the original forty-plus homes remained. Feeble and lacking spunk in their advanced age, the lingering inhabitants withered and crumbled along with the structures around them. Some of the final squatters died of exposure; a few of suicide; still others were discovered moribund in dilapidated ruins and carted away by the constable.

FINAL VESTIGES

The last known inhabitant of Dogtown was Cornelius Finson, or "Black Neil," a former slave who was favored among the witches. As they died off or were deliriously escorted away, Finson remained, living among the undomesticated dogs, boarding himself up in the basement of a tottering old building, spending years fruitlessly rooting and excavating for what he believed was buried treasure. In 1830, he was discovered frost-bitten, wrapped in rags and spouting gibberish; the constable took him from the settlement to a poor house, where he died shortly thereafter.

With its miscreant and waylaid occupants mere ghosts among its ruins, Dogtown became ever denser and more untamed; Mother Nature, as they say, abhors a vacuum, and she quickly reclaimed her keep. In 1845, when a work crew was sent to bushwhack the old town paths and pull down what remained of the town's rotting structures, the area was further absorbed back into the wild.

Since then, the area has continued to attract a sinister and decidedly bizarre element. There have been various high-profile murders and suicides within the Dogtown forest, which is now a 3,600-acre expanse covering much of Cape Ann and preserved by the nonprofit Essex National Heritage Area. Adding a further aura of creepiness and whimsicality to the already intimidating woods, some mischievous hands have placed what some have dubbed a stuffed animal graveyard—either that or a bizarre art installation. Beanie Babies, teddy bears, baby dolls, hand puppets and other miscellaneous cloth effigies have been both hung and placed in various parts of the straggling forest, serving as further evidence of the inspiration imbued by abandoned places.

Then there are the perplexing stories of those who for one reason or another, to their detriment, are drawn to Dogtown.

Retired fisherman James Merry, for instance, was an aspiring matador. He was said to have practiced wrestling with a bull calf that he pastured in a field near the former home of infamous Dogtowner, Easter Carter (a healer known for her wiles when it came to herbs and the special boiled cabbage dinners she put on for local youths). As it grew, however, the bull became ever more difficult for Merry to wrangle. In 1892, his body was discovered gored and smashed upon rocks; a simple stone marker now memorializes him.

Even today, walking within Dogtown's expansive depths can give one a feeling of unease. Although a trail head off Reynard Street offers a map, the sprawling area is labyrinthine, not well-marked, and easy to get turned around in. The first jarring detail is the persistent cadence of gunshots; the woods abut a shooting range, the rhythm of gunfire sending rhythmic exclamation points through the air. Passing over gravel that squeaks and squelches beneath sneaker soles, the bisecting trails lead through copses of trees, along a reservoir, sometimes diverting through openings awash with sunlight, other times dead ending at chain-link fences abutting backyards. Birds caw and serenade one another, bugs whiz about in their busy but aimless way, birches curve overhead like arches, charred scatterings of stones and disfigured and smashed beer bottles serve as remnants of recent festivities in these old woods.

Down a path several paces are the vestiges of the doomed settlement's one-time center, identified with a rock stamped with "D.T.S.Q." Diverting tracks run past the remains of cellar holes that are ruinous with time; like a scavenger hunt of sorts, some are easily identifiable immediately in the adjoining woods, others are hidden deep and indiscernible among other random, numerous jumbles and jetties of lichen-covered rocks. Passers-by can imagine the shambling shacks that stood here centuries ago, their hosts beckoning with their charms, portents, and potions.

As a sort of Puritan-esque antithesis to such anticipated visions of unbridled depravity that once reigned supreme here, a series of several dozen boulders stand stately and pious along one stretch of trail, asserting inspirational and positive messages and advice for good, clean, successful living. Certainly, jarring and out-of-place for the unsuspecting, they are the design of mid-twentieth century financial guru, writer, real estate developer, and one-time presidential candidate Roger W. Babson, a Gloucester native. Purchasing 1,150 acres of the former Dogtown woods in 1929, the founder of his namesake private Babson College in Wellesley was able to locate and mark several of the village's former homes and released one of the first historical pamphlets on the area as a result.

As a means of promoting encouragement and good spirit during the somber tidings of the Great Depression, he hired several unemployed stonecutters to carve sayings into several dozen rocks along what is now the forest's Babson Boulder Trail. In raised-relief lettering, they proclaim, "Be on Time," "Study," "Work," "Use Your Head," and espouse such virtues as "Initiative," "Integrity," "Intelligence," and "Courage." One of the largest and most imposing, meanwhile, standing at least fifteen feet high, simply declares, "Spiritual Power." (We can only assume that this affirmation would set Younger's purported evil eye rolling.)

Sporadic, ranging in size and scope, some situated several paces off the path and others facing away from it, identifying the marked boulders requires a bit of a quest, as well as a few diversionary jaunts. Snug among their midst is the local geographic oddity, "Whales Jaw" (or, at least, what remains of it), a giant rock formation that dates to the Pleistocene Era. In place for at least 10,000 years, it was given the fitting name—based on Gloucester's maritime heritage and thriving whale-watching tourism—because it resembled the enormous open jaws of a breaching sperm whale. Emblazoned with bits of graffiti that have been scrubbed away by hands and time only to be replaced by the scrawling of ensuing generations, the characteristic slab succumbed to gravity when a big hunk broke off in 1989, according to the town.

Ultimately, though, such boulders as "Whales Jaw" that were shaped by geography, as well as those etched by human hands, stand as a testament to the peculiar quality of this ancient place, a mystique that endures.

Twelve

HOPKINTON

Hope (Doesn't) Spring Eternal

A NARROW PATH, CROWDED BY PINES AND BIRCHES AND CAR-
peted with brown needles, runs like a seam between two houses.
After a few hundred steps, this opens to a clearing and a wide,
moss-covered bridge that spans a trickling brook.

It seems an unassuming location tucked in the woods off a sub-
division in Hopkinton—a tidy suburb in Massachusetts' thriving
"Metrowest" region roughly thirty miles west of Boston—but it
was once the site of a nationally renowned attraction.

Almost two centuries ago, Hopkinton was a premier resort
destination. For nearly four decades in the early 1800s, the Hopkinton Springs complex drew prestigious visitors from all over the
country and beyond. Presidents, senators, millionaire businessmen,
high-society types—they all came to bathe in or drink from its
three mineral springs known for their relaxation benefit and purportedly mystical healing waters.

As celebrated as the spa was, though, it is now a faded imprint
from Hopkinton's past. Hardly any signs of the once-flourishing
operation remain visible for modern visitors. The springs are lost;
the resort buildings razed and burned.

"It's like a haunted site," said Russ Greve, curator of the Hop-kinton Historical Society. As the tale goes, in 1815, a tornado and electrical disturbance known notoriously as "the great blow" ripped up trees and bulldozed all manner of buildings, including a sawmill owned by Joel Norcross.

When the raging storm abated and the calm returned, Nor-cross set to rebuilding his mill, and in the process came upon three springs, all within a short radius. Tests from a Boston doctor found them to be rich with magnesium, iron, and sulfur. Norcross deserted the hard, dangerous labor of operating a sawmill, instead opting for a more extravagant vocation. He immediately began entertaining visitors, and erected a thirty-nine room, four-story luxury hotel that accommodated up to 100 guests, according to local historian Gordon E. Hopper. It was also outfitted with a network of balconies, bowling alleys, and a dancing hall. Else-where, there were gazebos, and a grotto where water from the springs was served from faucets. At the wells tinged with iron and sulfur, shelters were raised, and guests were provided with seats and drinking cups.

The magnesium spring, though, was granted the most prom-inence. The largest of the three, it was accented by a large bath house and a stone fountain. To make its waters more comfortable for bathers, it was also heated by a system of flues and conduits, according to Gail Clifford, an amateur historian who has researched this lavish bit of her hometown's past. "He saw something natural and said, 'I can capitalize on that,'" Clifford said of Norcross. "He created an economy, made the lake a little special."

The key selling point: healing. The waters that gushed forth were publicized as "impregnated with minerals of great medicinal value." The marketing plan worked. Visitors arrived in throngs. First by horse-drawn coach, according to Hopper, then by rumbling steam engine after the Boston & Worcester Railroad reached Westborough in 1834.

There were pilgrimages from every New England state, as well as New York, Virginia, South Carolina, Kentucky, Louisiana, and Texas, according to a copy of the hotel log kept in the Hopkinton Public Library's archives. (The log cites a few curious locales, too, including "Phillidophia," "Cincinniata" and "Jerasalem.")

Lore about the springs fueled this renown. One story recalled how a man in the early stages of "consumption" (tuberculosis) took a dip in the springs and came home "completely cured," as described in John Hayward's 1839 *New England Gazetteer*.

"It put us on the map," Greve said of Norcross's enterprise. "It was a destination."

And the guests, accordingly, included some of the most distinguished of their time—and icons of modern generations.

On September 27, 1834, for instance, President Andrew Jackson purportedly made a visit, accompanied by his vice president and successor, Martin Van Buren (the mysterious phrase "O how mad he would be" accompanying their names in the log). Also making appearances were longtime U.S. senator and secretary of state Daniel Webster, who felt the need to remind those reading the register that he was "from Washington," U.S. Attorney General Ebenezer Rockwood Hoar, and Edward Everett, Massachusetts governor and U.S. senator.

There was a rotating assembly of aristocrats and hoi polloi, too: The log has Forbeses, Grants, Starkweathers, Varneys, Hurds, and Barkers dishing out $1 per day or $10 a week.

And in the records, they gushed about the price—"25 cents for a bath (well worth the money)"—and lamented leaving: "My stay is short." Female companions, meanwhile, were typically left anonymous, and listed like pieces of baggage: Benjamin Richardson, for example, came with his "wife and mother, daughter and cousin," while "E.B. Fay & 6 Ladies" and "S.H. Brown & 4 Ladies" arrived on the same day in July 1835. Other guests hid behind pseudonyms, or vagaries: "Icabod Crane" came from "Capertown," "Uncle Joshua" made the trek from "Way Down East," and "Nameless and his lady" visited from "Nothing town," all in the summer of 1836.

But such visitors, if arriving today, would be surprised to find their destination is the "nothing town." After the hotel abruptly closed in 1859—Norcross, it was said, was bankrupt, in failing health, and crushed by the recent loss of his wife—the property was sold, and it fell into neglect; the outbuildings were razed, and the hotel ultimately destroyed by fire, according to numerous accounts.

Today, all that remains is a scattering of unusual formations and bridges in the woods, and fragments of history in newspaper articles and research papers. There are no known original pictures. And the springs, if they still flow, are no longer visible. They may have been engulfed by the rising lake waters when Whitehall Reservoir was established. However, their ultimate fate is uncertain; neither the state Department of Conservation and Recreation nor the town's Conservation Commission has researched whether they still exist.

The only certainty is that, as the days tumbled over days, the decades flowed over decades, the earth imposed her will on the topography of the land, water, and springs. Perhaps someday they will grandeur once again.

THIRTEEN

THE BERKSHIRES
Beautiful Mysteries

LOCATED IN THE FAR WESTERN CORNER OF MASSACHUSETTS bordering New York State, the Berkshires are known for their rurality, pristineness, quaintly New England villages and towns, farm-to-table sentimentality, abundant recreational opportunities, and vibrant arts culture comprising of museums, nationally renowned music venues and popular festivals. A beloved tourism destination that is part of the Northeast Appalachians, the area holds historical significance, as well: During the American Revolution, Henry Knox and his troops hauled cannons captured at Fort Ticonderoga through its rugged, uneven hills en route to Boston.

Sparsely populated now as it was centuries ago, the region also cloaks ghost towns within its wooded wilds.

DAVIS
Around the beginning of the second Industrial Revolution, sulfuric acid became a critical commodity for commercial purposes. It is used to produce other chemicals, as well as glue and explosives, and aids in the curing of metal and the refinement of petroleum.

Luckily for locals, in the late 1880s, an abundant outcropping of iron pyrite was discovered in the hills between the small towns of Rowe and Charlemont off the Native American trade route the Mohawk Trail. Popularly known as "fool's gold," pyrite can be processed to yield sulfide, which in turn is used to manufacture sulfuric acid.

Wasting no time in capitalizing on the need for the substance and its integral components, Herbert J. Davis established a mine in the area around 1882. His H. J. Davis Company soon burrowed four shafts that excavated nearly pure, coarse-granular, shiny yellow pyrite. It became the state's largest iron pyrite mine at the time, reaching daily shipments of up to 150 tons at its height. The operation also yielded smaller amounts of copper.

Once it was up and running, the village of Davis grew up quickly around it. This hamlet eventually boasted 150 homes, as well as a blacksmith and butcher shop. To support the mine, there was also a shaft house, a tram, and a large reduction building complete with a massive smokestack. Ahead of its time in more than one respect, Davis and the surrounding area also had electricity—in fact, nearby Charlemont claimed to be the first in the state to be electrified. This not only helped improve the quality of life but was used to light the mine for increased efficiency and productivity. Workers were said to be paid handsome wages for the time: between $12 and $15 a day.

The operations provided a significant, much needed economic boon for both Rowe and Charlemont. The latter southern town had a limited industrial base comprised of a few sawmills, handle shops, and chairmaking operations. With the Davis mine running at full speed, Charlemont was able to open and sustain a rake handle shop and a carriage shop (which also produced wooden spools for the silk mills churning away in Northampton to the south). Local farmers also benefitted; they supplied the mine with abundant timber and firewood and sold provisions including fruits, vegetables, and dairy products to workers, visitors, and passers-through. The mine at Davis even became a tourist attraction, featuring an observation tower above its main shaft that offered sweeping views of its workers, shops, state-of-the-art lighting, and horse-drawn wagons hauling pyrite and coal.

But economic calamity struck in 1911 when the mine experienced a cave-in blamed on poor mining practices. Luckily, there were no deaths and just limited injuries, but operations never rebounded. With opportunities limited due to decreased production, workers and their families began to move away. By the mid-1930s, the former bustling village was reduced to a mishmash of cellar holes, a crumbling blacksmith shop, and a deteriorating smokestack. Its sparse remnants are now located on private land in Rowe, which eventually absorbed the abandoned village.

However, the site now serves an important ecological purpose: It is a significant study area for the University of Massachusetts—Amherst. When the mine collapsed, it began seeping groundwater from its workings into a downhill creek. Common at abandoned mine sites, this is what's known as acid mine drainage, and it is characterized by high levels of metals and low pH. While researchers in the fields of microbiology, geology, engineering, and science have emphasized that there is no threat to water supplies or the environment—the iron sulfide in the mine has few hazardous impurities—they consider the site important when it comes to bioremediation. Study has focused on natural drainage processes and how the mine's slow purification over time, which could ultimately enable quicker cleanups in similar situations elsewhere.

So, in its demise, Davis serves a significant higher purpose.

CATAMOUNT

With the passage of time and shifting trends in economics, some towns simply become obsolete and uninhabitable. Such was the case with Catamount, a tiny village in Colrain in northwestern Massachusetts bordering Vermont.

It existed from the mid-1700s to the late-1800s and was mainly a farming community. It also had a small tourism cottage industry, as the nearby Pocumtuck Mountain was a popular seasonal destination, and residents held a regular Old Home Days festival there that even attracted Massachusetts Governor John Davis Long in 1880. But the town's true claim to fame (and a fact that was established in the history books, if but as a footnote) is that its schoolhouse was the first in the nation to fly the American flag. Other than that, not much is known about life in the small hamlet in the woods.

Due largely to that remote, rugged location—and with the local farming industry waning due to larger-scale production methods—Catamount was abandoned by the early 1900s. The state acquired a large chunk of it in 1967 and established the Catamount State Forest, which today features hiking trails and other recreational opportunities.

There is also a stone marker commemorating its small place in history: "The first U.S. flag raised over a public school was floated in May 1812 from a log schoolhouse which stood on this spot." The marker names its makers as Mrs. Rhoda Shippee, Mrs. Lois Shippee, Mrs. Sophia Willis, and Mrs. Stephen Hale, and notes that it was raised by Amasa Shippee, Paul Davenport, "and the loyal families of Catamount Hill."

And although not much is left but for the occasional foundation or stone wall hidden deep in the woods, visitors do from time-to-time plant small American flags in the ground in homage to those loyal families.

QUESTING

It's a unique and curious name for a long-abandoned colonial settlement of which just bits and pieces of history remain. Located in present-day New Marlborough in the southeast corner of Massachusetts, it was graced with that dignified moniker by its longtime twentieth century owners, Dr. Robert Lehman and his wife Janet Fraser Lehman.

In Arthurian legend, the knights of the Round Table, among their many other pursuits, sought to kill the Questing Beast, a creature with the body of a leopard, the neck of a snake, the feet of a rabbit and the rear of a lion. Fans of the fabled tales, the Lehmans sought to reflect their own "quest" to restore the original property and the lands surrounding it.

What little is known about the present-day nature preserve and site of the original New Marlborough settlement is that it hosted the area's first fort (placed at its highest ridge and storing gunpowder) and welcomed its first non-Native American children, the Brookins twins. The precise location of this settlement has been lost to time, but the subsequent location saw the clearing of much of its forest. In the mid-1800s, brothers William and Jerome Leffingwell farmed the land. Unfortunately, both were killed in farming accidents, and the settlement was abandoned by the Great Depression. It eventually passed into the hands of Robert Lehman, a prominent pharmacologist who developed drugs to treat, among other disease, heart failure and glaucoma. Over the years, he and his wife bought up as much of the surrounding land as they could, which was then bequeathed to The Trustees of Reservations in 1996.

Today, the only remnants of the 438-acre property's long and largely mysterious history are cellar holes and stone walls, ruins of the Leffingwell farmstead and barn. Preserved for the ages, the reservation is today a mix of hardwood forests, wetlands, streams, vernal pools, and wildflower fields traced with nature paths. Now as in its near and distant past, it invites visitors to pursue their own "quests."

Part III

New Hampshire

And this story, having no beginning, will have no end.
—Clive Barker, Weaveworld

The Granite State is one of divergent personalities. On the one hand, it can seem a wild frontier of sorts—nearly all of its northern section is taken up by the sprawling White Mountain National Forest. On the other, its southern half is thickly settled and referred to by some as a suburb of Massachusetts. But speckled across its triangular expanse are also quaint villages, rural farms—and abandoned towns that have been either cherished and preserved for the ages, swallowed by lakes and reservoirs, or nearly forgotten to time and left to the elements.

Fourteen

MONSON

Briefly, A Community—Then Preserved

Walk down a narrow, tree-lined dirt lane that isn't quite backcountry enough to be just a walking trail, but isn't substantial enough to be a road, either (at least by today's standards). In this case, it appears just right as you pass through an enclosed grove of trees lined with moss-layered rocks and carpets of pine needles.

After a few hundred yards, the overarching trees open up and give way to verdant fields on both sides traced by rock walls. There are birdhouses and informational placards, as well, and up ahead, a humble, rectangular Colonial-era house of muted green. The trail rambles on beyond more forest and meadows dappled with wild-flowers, 250-year-old cellar holes and rock walls, and a lily-padded pond with beaver lodges and herons posed like lithe statues.

This is the former town of Monson, New Hampshire. And, while it may not look exactly as it did when it existed for a brief thirty-some-odd years back in the 1700s, it's likely as close as it's going to get for the twenty-first century.

Monson is unique in that it may have been abandoned—but it has not been forgotten. In fact, quite the contrary. An effort by concerned community members in the 1990s has helped ensure it for posterity.

The tiny hamlet marks history as the state's first inland colony. As other settlers clustered around New Hampshire's small slice of the Atlantic coast or along the gushing waters of the Merrimack and Nashua rivers, a small group of settlers established a farming community near present-day Hollis, Milford, and Brookline on the Massachusetts border. In fact, the 17,000-acre settlement was initially part of the state to the south until Colonial border lines were adjusted in 1741.

The town's founders hailed from the Bay State and Nova Scotia; they purchased the land in 1735, then moved there in 1737, clearing woods, blazing walking paths, and building a cluster of homes. It was a humble existence: There was no schoolhouse, church, or meeting hall, and the only town property was described as a "pound for unruly cows."

Still, Monson had a few good decades and at its height had a population of 293, according to Census figures. Its residents over its short time span included members of the Nevins, Hopkins, Colburn, Kendrick, Hutchinson, Leeman, Taylor, Gould, and Wallingford families. Some of the more colorful town figures included William Nevins, a twice-married father of nine who was a longtime moderator and selectman; Dr. John Brown, a respected physician who drew looks from everyone around with his chaise carriage; and Joshua Bailey, a pater familias to eleven children whose house burned down (everyone escaped).

But secluded, inland life under provincial rule proved to be too much. In 1763, just a quarter-century after it was settled, the town petitioned to be excused from paying province taxes. At the time, there were twenty-one households, and the entreaty stated that they were living very plainly and with difficulty. There were also continuous border contentions with Hollis and other surrounding towns. Furthermore, several pleas by Monson residents to build a school, meetinghouse, or church were not passed.

The petition was ignored, though, and by 1770, villagers had had enough. They once again petitioned the general court to dissolve their charter. Their stated reason: "That the Land in and about the Center of Monson is so very poor, Broken, Baron and uneven, as cannot admit of many Settlers, so that those Families that are in Town, are almost all planted in the Extreme parts of it. We have no prospect of ever Building a Meeting-House in the Center or elsewhere, any ways to accommodate us, by which Difficulties we think the Gospel will not be settled among us while in the present situation."

This time (perhaps conveniently for the grantors) their request was approved. Monson's acreage was divided up between Hollis, Milford, Brookline, and Amherst, and remaining families either moved away or became residents in one of those absorbing towns.

It was unusual for a town to request its own elimination—why would it give up on itself rather than stay and fight? (It was, after all, the period of the American Revolution when independent spirit and patriotism were broiling.)

More than 250 years later, the reasons are still debated.

Russ Dickerman, the great-great-great-grandson to one of the town's founders Richard Clark, and whose family has owned property in the area since the 1730s, has said it was the culmination of a number of adverse factors. These included poor town planning, an unforgiving landscape, clashes with indigenous people, and a tax structure that benefited non-resident landowners.

Notably, Dickerman has pointed to political greed, particularly on the part of Benning Wentworth, governor of the province of New Hampshire from 1741 to 1766. Wentworth turned down every petition Monson residents put before him, and along with King George III, focused on increasing his own land holdings through unequal taxation. Had he wanted communities to flourish, Dickerman has contended, Wentworth would have helped establish infrastructure in and between them. Similarly, George III wanted province taxes paid in silver, but he only authorized paper money in the colonies—so in many cases they simply couldn't pay.

But their ancestors, it seems, were much more inclined to rallying.

The former town had enjoyed a relative serenity of two-and-a-half centuries, sitting untouched and largely forgotten. But in 1998, a housing development of twenty-eight high-end townhouses was proposed. Dickerman and his late wife, Geri, immediately began a "Save Monson Center" campaign to garner community support. They also enlisted the help of state archaeologist Gary Hume, who touted the archaeological significance of the site—one of the foremost in New England, in fact. The Society for the Protection of New Hampshire Forests also got involved, as did the New Hampshire Division of Historical Resources, and Inherit New Hampshire (now the New Hampshire Preservation Alliance). All these were enlisted following passionate pleas by the Dickermans).

Within just six months' time, their combined forces raised $350,000 from more than 400 major donors. The Forest Society purchased the property in 1998, and now oversees it. The Dickermans, for their part, donated 205 acres of their own property. Underscoring community support, in 2008 the town of Milford required that the developer of a nearby subdivision configure its open space to abut the Monson reservation and donate those forty-seven acres to the Forest Society.

Now, the land that formerly comprised Monson and the town's historical heritage are preserved for perpetuity. The property extends more than 280 square miles across Hollis, Brookline, Amherst, and Milford. Ever Monson's greatest champion, Dickerman has served as its caretaker and official tour guide since its purchase. He even rebuilt the J. Gould House, the only remaining structure on the property. Dating to 1756, it was used as both a home and clock shop. This he turned into a museum filled with his own family's heirlooms, as well as numerous (and eclectic) relics from the town and the era. These include portraits, maps, an album full of letters and other documents, old garden tools and other implements, and clothing. There is also a stack of books on the paranormal, and a certificate from the local group Ghost Quest that declares the site officially haunted (it is a purported paranormal hotspot). A prolific woodcarver and handyman, Dickerman has also built the numerous birdhouses that line what was once Monson's main road, and carved tree trunk benches that run along its length.

Visitors to the property, if they've been lucky enough, have been greeted by him and learned of his own family story. Excepting a time between 1928 and 1955, Dickerman's family has owned property in Monson since the 1730s. His great-grandfather, Samuel Russell Dickerman, died at age thirty-six while a prisoner of the Confederate military in Andersonville, Georgia. His mother and father, who lived at opposite ends of Monson, married during the Great Depression. But with work scarce and neighbors and friends losing their houses, they relocated to Somerville. Dickerman was born there, but as he grew up, he abhorred city living, so he returned to the home of his ancestors.

Now, due largely to him, it is a haven for many others, as well. A short walk from a small dirt parking lot off Adams Road in Hollis brings visitors past a wooden "Monson Center" sign, then a small kiosk with a map of property trails and a brief history of the (brief) town. A little further along, as fields hemmed in by stone walls slope up and down on either side, is Dickerman's museum. The nature path, once the village's main street, leads back into the woods to a beaver pond. A slate stone tilting into the earth announces: "In this area lay the center of the old town of Monson 1746 to 1770." Another demarcates the site of the former town pound.

And spotted along the way are the foundations of the original mid-eighteenth century homes. These are identified with signs and offer colorful bits of history on their former inhabitants.

William Nevins Sr., for instance, was born in Nova Scotia and was engaged in "subduing the forests, making paths, fighting wild men and wild beasts." He was married twice (his first wife died), and over a period of twenty-four years, had nine children—six boys and three girls. Five of his sons served in the Revolutionary War. He was a man of "considerable influence" in town affairs, having served as moderator twenty-seven times and as a selectman for sixteen years.

His brother, Deacon Thomas Nevins Jr., was "born on the Atlantic Ocean" in March 1711. He moved to Monson before 1738, was married to Bridget Snow, had eight children, and served in the old French war as a sergeant. Also serving as a town selectman, Nevins Jr. "came within the limits of Hollis in 1770; removed to Hebron in 1772." That year, he served as juryman at the County Court held in Amherst. His name is attached to a "remonstrance against a petition Annex" of the easterly side of Cockermouth to Plymouth. We also learn that, "Late in life, he removed to Hanover, N.H., or near there, where he resided the remainder of his days."

There are also the former home sites of:

- Dr. John Brown, who was born in Rowley, Massachusetts, in 1724, and assisted his father in hotel keeping as a youth. He moved to Monson around 1750 and became the only physician Monson ever had, "so far as we have any account."

He was a veteran of the French and Indian War and served under Lieutenant Colonel John Goffe in the Crown Point expedition of 1757; locally, he was selectman from 1756 to 1758. A father of ten children—four boys and six girls—Brown was a grantee of Plymouth, New Hampshire, where he moved in 1766.

- Joshua Bailey, of Andover, Massachusetts, whose house caught fire one evening when he was visiting his neighbor, Mr. Gould, the town clock maker. His children escaped the fire in their nightclothes. The house was not rebuilt, and the family soon went "west with the Mormons."

- Richard Bayley, "the old Monson shoe cobbler," one of the early town settlers. He was a descendant of Richard Bayley, who came over from England in the ship *Bevins* in 1638 and settled in Salem, Massachusetts. He was "located in Monson" prior to 1760, a "plebian who helped to make up the population of the pioneer settlement." He used to take his bench and kit of tools and go house to house, "doing such making and repairing as each family might want."

- Lazarus Hubbard, "the beggar." Born in Hollis at the south part of Monson Village, he married, moved to nearby Antrim, then returned to Monson in 1801. "According to tradition, Mr. Hubbard was the poorest and laziest man that ever lived in this section," we learn. A noted beggar, he traveled from house to house, peddling medicinal herbs and nostrums and occasionally brooms peeled from witch hazel (in general use at the time among the farming community). He would, "as was the custom with some," hang his mop, broom, gridiron and frying pan on the outside of the house next to the entrance door. He disappeared from Monson prior to 1820.

- Lieutenant David Wallingsford, originally from Bradford, Massachusetts, and a descendant of Nicholas Wallingsford who emigrated from London to Boston on *The Confidence* in 1638. He came to Monson in 1765, where, like most residents, "he engaged in agricultural pursuits." He enlisted in the Revolutionary War under Captain Dow's company for Concord and Lexington and was at the Battle of Bunker Hill. He made lieutenant in Captain Archelaus Town's company at the Battle of Bennington and was one of the first to order his men to fire on the British and Hessians (German auxiliary soldiers). Unfortunately, as was all too common: "He was paid off in worthless Continental money at the close of the war and had the misfortune to lose his house by fire."

These historical tidbits punctuate the panorama of fields, flowers, and forest. All told, it is a peaceful and pastoral place—a fitting, living epilogue to Monson's story.

Fifteen

RELOCATED, INUNDATED

Damming up rivers, streams, and other water bodies has been a common occurrence throughout New England. Mill and factory owners practiced it to fuel early commerce and industry; state and local governments to sustain growing populaces or to prevent damaging floods.

And more often than not, it has meant the washing out of small towns—as was the case with the New Hampshire villages of Old Hill and East Weare.

THE PROMISE OF HIGHER GROUND

In the late 1930s, the residents of Old Hill Village learned of their troubling fate: Their roughly 185-year-old town was to become the site of a flood control reservoir for the Franklin Falls Dam project. Within just a few years, it would be directly in the path of—and eventually underneath—the dammed-up waters of the Pemigewasset River.

Unlike other towns literally liquidated for reservoir and dam projects, though, villagers weren't simply forced out and scattered. They had the novel idea to rebuild on higher ground and relocate as an entire community.

Incorporated in 1754 as New Chester, the village had a long relationship with water both beneficial and detrimental. To start, it was located just east of modern-day Manchester on the banks of the Pemigewasset, a water body that initially helped fuel its growth. It was first granted to several local men as part of a 30,000-acre speculation purchase.

Settlers built homesteads over the ensuing decades, and ferry service across the Pemigewasset was established at the turn of the nineteenth century. In the 1830s, the residents of the now busy town learned that there were dozens of other communities across the country with the name "Chester." Reflecting their pride in their community and their state, they renamed the town "Hill" in 1837 after then-Governor Isaac Hill.

The village continued to grow, with residents tending farms on the surrounding countryside and working at stores and mills in adjacent towns including Bristol and Franklin. Hill was further bolstered by the arrival of the railroad along the banks of the river. This served as a major source of both public transportation and shipping. The town was also connected to nearby Sanbornton by covered bridge. Spanning the Pemigewasset, it was 150 feet long and thirty feet wide. With the arrival of the automobile in the early twentieth century, a sign on the bridge cautioned drivers not to go faster than a person could walk—lest they pay a fine of $5.

Interestingly, Hill was also for a brief period host to a hydrotherapy resort. Between 1859 and 1870, Dr. William Vail ran his Granite State Health Institute out of a grand brick building on Main Street. Boarders paid between $5 and $9 a week to take long baths in pure water or to be wrapped for hours in damp cloths. Hydropathy or "water cure," which dates as far back as ancient Egypt, had a modern revival in the nineteenth century. It was touted not only for its cleansing properties, but for its treatment of pain—as well as its ability to "rouse the soul." Visitors to the Institute included Christian Science Church founder Mary Baker Eddy. The source for "the cure" in Hill was the spring that fed the entire town.

But in other cases, and long before it was wiped out by it, water was not at all a cure for Hill itself—it was a destructive force. The Pemigewasset was a major tributary of the Merrimack River, and it was prone to frequent flooding because it carried off melting snow from the northern White Mountains. The area was consumed by devastating floods in 1875, 1916, and 1936. The 1875 inundation, when the Pemigewasset reportedly rose thirty feet above its banks, drowned cattle and damaged lowlands. Meanwhile, in 1913, ice lifted the covered bridge between Sanbornton and Hill off its abutments and carried it downriver. To ensure that it didn't cause further damage downstream, it was dragged to shore and burned.

By the 1930s, the government decided to take action. In 1938, the year of the Great New England Hurricane—one of the most destructive and powerful in recorded history to hit the region—the U.S. Army Corps of Engineers informed Hill residents that they would have to move. The Franklin Falls dam was being built to control flood waters in the Merrimack River basin.

It was startling news, to be sure, but by January 1940, Hill residents formed an association, purchased land, and began planning a new village modeled on the old. This was located on higher ground to the west. Construction began that same year, and in just a few months, a new town hall, school, nearly three dozen houses, and street and water systems were completed. Fourteen buildings were salvaged from "Old Hill," as it was now referred to; these were moved upland via winch and horse teams.

Making the move official, a town meeting was called in 1941 in the old town hall, then recessed and reconvened at the new town building. Old Hill Village was no more.

The $7.9 million dam was completed in 1943. It stands a commanding 140 feet tall and spans three-quarters of a mile across the Pemigewasset. Maintained by the U.S. Army Corps of Engineers, it drains a 1,000 square-mile watershed extending all the way to the White Mountains and is capable of controlling more than 50 billion gallons of water. The 3,900-acre Franklin Falls reservoir around it is now a recreation area managed by the state.

Few traces of the old village remain, as all structures had to be razed to ensure that there was no manmade debris in the dam impoundment area. Those who walk the Old Hill Village Trail will come upon several crumbling, mossed-over foundations and retaining walls; some rusted sewer pipes, railings, and barbwire fences; and fallen-down stone steps and barely-there sidewalks leading off into the forest depths.

The new Hill, meanwhile, sits perched at its upland location—free, at last, of any encroaching waters.

FLOODS OF CHANGE

Although it existed for more than 200 years, little remains of East Weare Village, either physically or in documentation. The one commemoration of the washed away town is a road marker on a lonely section of Route 77 in its sister town of Weare that describes the "sacrifice" of "their beautiful community" as part of the Hopkinton-Everett Lakes Flood Risk Management Project.

Located southwest of the capital seat of Concord and northwest of Manchester, the area that would come to be Weare was initially a grant by Massachusetts Colonial Governor Jonathan Belcher. It was first known as Beverly-Canada, then Halestown,

Robiestown, and Wearestown, reflecting the ebb and flow of settlement. Finally, in 1764, it was declared Weare in honor of first New Hampshire "president," Meshech Weare ("president" being the precursive name to "governor"). Weare was also known as "The Father of New Hampshire."

The earliest settlers built rustic cabins along the banks of the Piscataquog River and farmed, hunted, fished, and harvested wood. By the early 1900s, nearly two dozen small mills were spotted along the waterway in Weare and East Weare. At its peak, East Weare was home to sixty families and was a "self-supporting thriving community," as noted on New Hampshire Historic Marker No. 143. "Farming and lumbering was the way of life for the villagers."

The village also had a train depot for the Boston & Maine Railroad, as well as a school, post office, garage, grocery store, lumber mills and a gristmill, Grange Hall, creamery, blacksmith shop, churches, and cemeteries—even a toy shop. But as with many small inland New England towns, it felt the effects of the Industrial Revolution and the Great Depression: Large woolen and cotton mills and shoe factories were thrumming in Manchester and other surrounding cities; grain was being imported in bulk (and much more cheaply) from the west; and plastic products were coming into vogue (thus replacing wooden ones).

Then there were the destructive floods that hit with increasing regularity. In November 1927, rivers and streams across New England, including the 117-mile Merrimack River and its tributaries, overflowed, claiming several lives and causing rampant damage. Then, just nine years later, the worst flood in three centuries inundated the eastern and central United States. In New England, twenty-four people died, 77,000 were left homeless, and losses exceeded $36 million, according to the U.S. Army Corps of Engineers.

New Hampshire and Massachusetts set to literal and figurative damage control, initiating a plan to minimize the Merrimack River Basin's calamitous flooding potential. In June 1938, Congress approved construction of a two-dam system along the Piscataquog and Contoocook rivers in New Hampshire. The Hopkinton-Everett dams, once finished, would help ensure that communities throughout central and southern New Hampshire and northern Massachusetts would not suffer such devastation again (that was, except for Weare).

Then, yet again, the area was stunned—this time by the Great New England Hurricane in September 1938, which consumed lives, buildings, and land all at once. This was barely three months after the federal government approved the damming project.

The village of East Weare learned that it would be displaced by the project and the rivers' rising waters; residents were bought out and relocated throughout the surrounding area. Also moved were portions of several state highways and utilities, an abandoned railroad, and four cemeteries. An interstate compact was approved in 1957 and construction of the Hopkinton dam on the Contoocook and the Everett dam on the Piscataquog began in 1959. They were completed in 1962 at a cost of $21.5 million. The massive system, which also includes diversion canals, provides flood protection to downstream residential, commercial, and industrial property. According to the U.S. Army Corps of Engineers, it has prevented hundreds of millions in flood damages.

The sacrifice of East Weare a small price to pay in return?

SIXTEEN

THE WHITE MOUNTAINS

Towns Untamed

COMPRISING ROUGHLY 800,000 ACRES ACROSS THE BORDERS OF New Hampshire and Maine, the White Mountain wilderness is a beloved national forest. Taking up nearly all of northern New Hampshire and a sizable chunk of southwestern Maine, the region attracts millions of people a year from all over the world.

They converge on the area to hike thousands of miles of trails traversing bumps, ridges, hills, and mountainous peaks named by long ago exiled natives, or in honor of U.S. presidents—the apex being the area's grand Mount Washington standing 6,288 feet. They scale rock faces; paddle, swim and fish lakes, ponds, and mountain-chilled streams and falls; ski and snowboard; ride historic cog railways and drive scenic routes including the Kancamagus Highway (or "The Kanc"). Or, simply, they revel in the pristine, fresh-aired, clean-skied, rugged natural beauty of the region, whether it be lush with green, swathed in snow, or ablaze with autumn color.

Even at their calmest, though, the White Mountains can be harsh, even cruel—many have entered them and disappeared, absorbed by their vastness. Conversely, others have tried and failed to tame them with farms or to otherwise strip them of their resources. This is evidenced by the many ghost towns hidden deep within the national forest's byzantine wilds or humbly dappled along its borders and foothills.

Naturally for its abundance of both hardwood and softwood trees, raging rivers, and mineral and ore deposits, New Hampshire once had busy logging, milling, and mining economies. Although it's hard to tell now that these sites were ever there—the forest has largely taken back its own over the last 150 years.

In most cases, because they existed on what is now federally protected land, these long-lost towns are truly ghosts in every sense of the word: They were either dismantled upon their abandonment or their remains reclaimed by nature, the land they once dominated never to be touched again by human development. Similarly, the same life cycles played out throughout their often minimally recorded histories: They were quickly settled and developed to reap maximum profits. Railroads were laid down through and around them and connected to the many other miles of circuitous tracks whose railcars were stacked with crude and virgin products for the next step in production. But then often came floods, storms, and fires—consuming blazes being all too common in the early mill days because they were hastily built wooden structures and safety practices were often lax. Not to mention they were filled with (and surrounded by) lumber, which only served to stoke the flames. Most significantly, logging towns, by their very nature, quickly brought about their own demise because they dwindled the very resources that initially made them prosper. So, just as quickly as they sprang up, they were just as promptly abandoned.

As such, lumbering villages tend to be unique from other New England ghost towns because not much remains of their human histories—the men, women, and children who lived there; the daily goings-on of home, work, school, and recreation; their memories, if brief, of how they got there and where they moved on to.

Nevertheless, we can always learn from history, so theirs should also be told.

PASSACONAWAY

One of the largest and most prosperous former logging towns was likely Passaconaway, located in present-day Albany in the southeastern corner of the White Mountains (near the tourist mecca of Conway). It was originally known as the Albany Intervale, but its name now honors a seventeenth century "sachem" (head chief) and later a "bashaba" (chief of chiefs). Passaconaway was legendary for his so-called mystical powers, as well as his ability to keep peace with the white man and bring together his own people. Notably, he refused to fight with European settlers upon the commandment of the "Great Spirit," and he founded what's known as the Pennacook Confederacy, a large community of nearly two dozen local tribes. This peacekeeping mentality was carried forward by his son, Wonalancet, but not by his grandson, Kancamagus—who gave his name to the byway that wends fifty-nine scenic miles east-to-west across northern New Hampshire.

As was custom at the time, early settlers hunted, trapped, and farmed. The Annis family was one of the first to establish a homestead on a site cleared in the 1790s (and their ancestors remained in the area until the Great Depression years). In those first days, Patriarch Joseph and his son Jim drove a stagecoach the several miles to and from Conway bringing mail, passengers, and tourists. Other early families included the Shackfords, farmers who encouraged earlier tourism by taking in boarders looking for hiking, fishing, and hunting opportunities; Thomas Russell and his sons, who built the Albany covered bridge; Jack Allen, a trapper and guide for post-Civil War tourists; and homestead namesake Ruth Priscilla (Russell) Colbath.

The Albany Intervale area was recognized early on for its lumbering prospects and was the site of three early settlements: Haskell's, Allen's Mill, and Quint's. These weren't supported by railroads, but they encompassed mills (likely for bobbins), boarding houses, stables, barns, and a blacksmith shop.

The Bartlett Lumber Company operated a short-lived logging operation and railroad in the otherwise agricultural-subsisting community from 1887 to 1894; then the Conway Lumber Company built the twenty-six-mile Swift River Railroad, and in short time, two other railroads that carried timber from its large stands of virgin lumber around the region to its mill in Conway village. This was one of New England's largest sawmills, comprising a 20,000-square-foot, three-story, steel frame building with surrounding kindling and box mills, several sheds, and a steam-headed log pond. The complex was state-of-the-art for its time, using waste wood for fuel.

At the height of logging operations, Passaconaway was believed to have around 1,500 residents living in several boarding houses and small homes, sending their children to several town schools, and frequenting a lumber store, company store, and post office (this in operation from 1892 until 1916). Conway Lumber used the town's hotel, the Carrigain House, as its headquarters.

But by 1916, the area had been logged to its potential, and the company relocated its operations, railroad, and many of its workers to more economically propitious areas. Today, the circa-1831 Russell-Colbath Homestead is the last remnant of the town of Passaconaway. The simple colonial home was purchased by the U.S. Forest Service in 1969, has been restored and furnished, and is listed on the National Register of Historic Places—one of the few structures in the White Mountains to carry that distinction. It is now the centerpiece of a historic park with informative markers, a nature trail, and small cemetery.

Ruth Colbath, who lays there in her eternal rest, once lived in the home with her husband Thomas. According to local folklore, one night in 1891, Thomas left for what was to be a short interlude—but never returned. Ever faithful, Ruth kept a lit candle in the window every night. Until her death in 1930, she never remarried and supported herself with several small jobs, including farming and serving as postmistress of Passaconaway. Thomas, it was said, finally did return three years after her death; but after hearing she was gone, wandered away once more.

The home at which Ruth kept vigil serves as a fitting symbol of the abandoned town—and the hope that some cling to even when all seems lost.

LIVERMORE VILLAGE

If Passaconaway was one of the most significant economically of White Mountain logging towns, then Livermore Village was the one with the most "life." Although now mere ruins—albeit dramatic compared to those of its counterparts—this stretch of forest just west of Bartlett was a self-sufficient community made up of numerous families.

Its origins date to 1874, when the Grafton County Lumber Company was incorporated by several members of the Saunders family. The following year, the enterprising businessmen established the Swayer River Railroad and built their first mill on the land that the state officially incorporated as Livermore in 1876. The name was a nod to Samuel Livermore, a New Hampshire senator related to the Saunders by marriage. Workers were recruited and soon instructed to hold their first town meeting.

An early fire destroyed the first mill, but it was rebuilt. Construction of the logging railroad began in 1877. Initially, it extended roughly two miles from the main line of the Portland and Ogdensburg Railroad—but it would eventually run about eight miles into the forest. By 1878, the cleared area of town was about a half a square mile, and there were two mills and a charcoal kiln below the village. The principal mill was powered by a 150-horsepower steam engine, and five boilers churned away in a steam plant. The C. W. Saunders, a wood-burning locomotive, shuttled lumber in and out of town, stopping on a trestle above the Sawyer River.

Livermore was a true company town: As was the case with many logging operations that sprung up throughout the White Mountains and elsewhere in New England, the Saunders owned everything, including the company store. Workers were expected to do all their shopping there; credit was extended until payday.

It was estimated that the Saunders' spent $150,000 on construction of the mill complex and the town. And it was certainly a profitable endeavor: In 1880, for instance, the total value of lumber, lathes, and shingles was $44,000.

It was prospering with families, too. Unlike other logging operations where mere clinical records survive, Livermore's history as a community is more fleshed out, as it were. According to the 1880 Census, the town comprised of eighteen dwellings with 103 inhabitants. Fourteen of those eighteen homes had children. Roughly twenty to twenty-five residents worked in the mill, skilled laborers earning $1.75 a day and others making $1.25. Otherwise, to make ends meet, locals took in borders or worked as coal dealers.

Most Livermorians were French-Canadian Catholics. A priest occasionally visited the town to hold services. Surviving town records reference births, deaths, and marriages. They are often only listed dates and names, but they give an idea of the natural cycle of human life. For instance, according to the research of local historian Peter Crane:

- On June 20, 1877, Daniel Huntley was born. His father was listed as a blacksmith.
- On July 5, 1878, George Smart, 5 months old, died of a bowel complaint. That same year, another 22-year-old family member, Albert Smart, died of consumption (tuberculosis).
- In September 1878, Julia Lucy, the daughter of a woodsman, was wed to Eldon Boynton, who worked as a carpenter in town.
- In 1882, Richard Whitty, a brakeman on the railroad, died when he was run over by his train.
- In 1886, a falling tree killed Michael Guinan, a 30-year-old Irishman.

The town had a post office from 1881 to 1931, and the first postmaster was William Hull. By 1885, the town had a town clerk, selectmen, treasurer, and tax collector, and a school where two teachers taught twenty-eight students. James F. Morrow Jr. who attended the school while his father worked in Livermore in the early 1920s, provided historians with a document listing books that were used in instruction: There were 408 volumes and eighty-eight titles, including the typical reading, writing, and arithmetic manuals, as well as copies of *Robinson Crusoe*, *The Song of Hiawatha*, and *Tom Brown's School Days*.

But the turn of the twentieth century brought demographic changes to Livermore. Although the population remained steady at 101, only eleven households remained and just five families had children, according to Census records. Eight homes took in boarders—one even had twenty. By the 1910s, the mill complex comprised of an icehouse, engine house, powerhouse, blacksmith shop, store, storehouse, and large barn (this in addition to the mill, homes, and boarding house). The Saunders family lived in a sprawling mansion—with a wrap-around porch, rotundas, double chimneys, and multi-gabled roof that would have inspired Nathaniel Hawthorne—atop a hill beside the railroad tracks. The Census also lists town livestock property: forty-eight horses, three cows, and two hogs.

Existing photos from that era collected by James F. Morrow Jr., and historian Rick Russack depict daily life. A clutter of houses at the base of the mountains, massive piles of logs nearly as tall as the buildings. Oxen traversing a hilly, boulder-strewn "path." The tiny one-room schoolhouse and the tidier company store. Children sledding down the main road covered in snow. Workmen posing on that same dirt road, flanked by their humble, identical houses with scant porches and fences (and the Saunders compound dominating the background).

But fire continued to devastate buildings, including the mill in 1909 and 1918, and the Saunders mansion in 1909. Then came the destruction of the notorious rains and floods of 1927; this wreaked havoc and consumed lives throughout the region, including in Livermore, where the logging railroad and several bridges were wiped out by Mother Nature's wrath. Stymied by all this, the mill finally closed in 1928. Six years later, in 1934, the Saunders and the U.S. Forest Service agreed on a sale of $9 an acre. Whatever equipment was salvageable was auctioned off. A few families remained until they could no longer eke out livings, and the Saunders kept their mansion—until it, too, became a casualty of fire.

Then finally, in 1951, the town charter was revoked by the state. Livermore was officially a dead town.

Today, tumbledown rubble remains among the grown-up forest. They are revealed after a roughly two-mile walk up the former railroad bed off Sawyer River Road west of Bartlett. Most significantly, a ragged, moss-covered stone wall of the powerhouse reaches up craggily toward the sky, vying for domination among stands of birch trees. Pillars, believed to be part of a system that supplied water to residents, rise above the rushing river. A rusting cast iron safe lies on its side in a warren of crumbling foundations of the sawmill, mansion, homes, and schoolhouse.

Eventually, they, like the town, will recede into time.

PIKE

In the 1820s, a unique type of rock known as mica schist was discovered in the rises and dips of Haverhill (also in the northwestern White Mountain area). Known as a metamorphic rock, it was formed through intense heat and pressure generated when North America and Africa slammed together to create Pangea 275 million years ago. It is the primary material in whetstones, or sharpening stones, which are used in a variety of industries.

Haverhill resident Peter Noyes made the geologic find in 1821 and started sharpening his scythes with it—mica schist worked better than any other stone he had tried. Twenty years later, Isaac Pike, a lumber baron, set up business in the Haverhill area to take advantage of its fertile timberlands. He soon realized the opportunities (and value) of mica schist. His namesake Pike Company began quarrying and producing whetstones, and rapidly bought out the operations and quarries of competitors. It shipped its first load of whetstone to Europe in 1846.

The company continued expanding rapidly, bolstered by the coming of the railroad around the time of the Civil War. It would go on to become the world's largest producer of sharpening stones and has since been absorbed by Norton Abrasives. Founded in 1885 and based in Worcester, Massachusetts, Norton manufactures bench stones, waterstones, abrasive files and slips, and specialty sharpening stones.

The Pike monopoly soon resulted in the area sharing its name. By 1880, the mill complex included sawmills, large farms, a store, post office, two schools and a horse stable. The Pike family built a mansion, and established a boarding house, dormitory for women workers, and tenements for mill workers. Freight cars were picking up products at the mill daily. The company employed more than 250 workers. A 1901 article in the *White Mountain Republic Journal* described "a little village of more than 500 inhabitants" with a "fine department store," "a good hall," mills, a box factory, wheelwright and blacksmith shop, gristmill, hotel, livery stable and schoolhouse. A "temperance place," it had a library, long distance telephone, telegraph, and "six mails a day."

But the development of artificial abrasives by the Norton Company (now Norton Abrasives) at the turn of the twentieth century dramatically changed the industry. Pike Company and Norton Company eventually consolidated—but only after four generations of the Pike family grew rich off northern New Hampshire's mica schist deposits.

Ninety years on, Pike is only survived by a squat, dilapidated brick structure and accompanying smokestack—hardly belying its significant contribution to society.

LIVERMORE TRIPOLI CO.

Much like mica schist, another resource for abrasives was discovered in the Livermore area in the White Mountains' southeast corner (near Conway and Bartlett). This is diatomaceous earth, which was formed from the fossilized remains of prehistoric algae (known as diatoms). Millions of years ago, when these tiny aquatic plants died, their remains formed a sediment at the bottom of water bodies. Its silica component is a fine powder that is extremely porous, making it very hard. Over the years, it has realized a myriad of uses, notably for silver, jewelry, and metal polishing. But it has been applied in many other ways: for polishing of daguerreotype plates in the early days of photography; as a filtering agent in water purification systems, food processing and beer brewing; as a liquid absorbent, matting and anti-block agent, reinforcing filler, and thermal insulator; even as a stabilizing component of dynamite and an activator in blood clotting studies.

Recognizing its implications early on was Charles B. Henry, youngest son to timber magnate J. E. Henry (of whom we shall read more shortly). J. E. Henry and Sons owned thousands of acres and operated several sawmills, pulp and paper mills, and a logging railroad in the region. In 1912, the younger Henry bought twelve acres of land around East Pond in Livermore and established the Livermore Tripoli Company. It was one of only two mining companies of its kind in New England. The sale price was $1, and the seller was Publisher's Paper Company—one of the largest landowners in the region, with thousands of acres of forestland in the White Mountains. Publisher's Paper and J. E. Henry had a longstanding business relationship and formed a sort of duopoly in northern New Hampshire's lumbering industry.

Livermore Tripoli constructed a mill and several other buildings and took advantage of the proximity of the Woodstock and Thornton Gore Railroad. East Pond was dredged for diatomaceous earth, which was then transported to holding tanks and processed. This was time, manpower and resource intensive and involved drying, separating, crushing, and milling the sediment. Various grades of the finished product were sold by weight and dependent upon the amount of processing they required. According to historical records, the most expensive was $75 a ton.

Lucrative as it seemed at the start, though, Livermore Tripoli didn't last long in the endeavor—while there are no concrete accounts of the company's demise, the general consensus is that it was due to the highly involved process and technical issues in separating the diatomaceous earth from the water and numerous other sediments at the bottom of East Pond. The short-lived company was dissolved in 1919, its buildings left to disintegrate. And Charles Henry, who had invested a significant amount in the enterprise, died just three years later.

FRANCONIA IRON WORKS
Today, Franconia in the northwestern corner of the White Mountains is the location of the beloved Franconia Notch State Park, Cannon Mountain, and the Frost Place, the former home of its celebrated namesake poet Robert Frost. But in the nineteenth century, there were two iron works in town that smelted iron and produced items including stoves, machinery, bar iron, cooking ware, castings, ox chains, tire irons, shovels, and scythes.

High-grade iron ore was discovered in nearby Sugar Hill (part of Lisbon) in the 1790s. Quickly, two different enterprises were incorporated to capitalize on the find: The New Hampshire Iron Factory Company and the Haverhill and Franconia Iron Works. The former operated what was known as the "Lower Works"; the later what was referred to as the "Upper Works." They were located about a mile apart, and both contracted out their mining and had ore and locally harvested limestone shipped in. Charcoal was paramount to operations: 160 bushes of charcoal were required to smelt just one ton of ore.

According to various accounts of the time, the Lower Works owned roughly 5,450 acres, an iron furnace enclosed in a gambrel-roofed building, a farm, sawmill, gristmill, and storage buildings. This in addition to several houses for the workmen and miller, a tavern, cookhouse, blacksmith shop and two stores. In 1810, the company also had nearly 1,000 tons of ore, twenty tons of limestone, and 180,000 bushels of charcoal.

The Upper Works, meanwhile, had 240 acres, a forge, furnace, two warehouses, three massive barns, gristmills and sawmills, a blacksmith shop, store, and six dwelling houses.

The two companies combined employed ninety men and had an annual payroll of $8,000. Most of what they produced was sold locally.

Little else is known of their operations or the men who worked in their factories and lived in their boarding houses. Similarly, there are conflicting reports of when they both ceased operations—likely after the close of the Civil War when ore deposits and lumber sources became diminished and cheaper iron was produced in the south. This lack of clarity in their timelines and histories is likely due to the fact that both ironworks changed hands a handful of times throughout the nineteenth century.

What is known is that the New Hampshire Iron Factory Company rebuilt its original furnace several times—and it still stands today at the far end of the Gale River, part of the town of Franconia's Besaw Iron Furnace Interpretive Center. An octagon standing a commanding thirty-two feet tall, it was crafted of local granite and lined with firebrick and clay. Chiseled into a heavy stone on its west arch is "S. Pettee Jr. 1859." The well-known iron master built several blast furnaces across New England and was the last known foreman at the Lower Works. It is the only blast furnace still standing in New Hampshire, a testament to a bygone era.

ZEALAND

Today the name is associated with a 4,300-foot-tall mountain, a notched mountain pass, a pond, a waterfall, and an Appalachian Mountain Club hut—all beloved destinations crossing the towns of Bethlehem and Lincoln at the northwestern border of the national forest.

But in the 1880s, a town named Zealand had a brief boom and bust as a lumbering community. Located within the township of Carroll not far from the zigzagging New Hampshire-Vermont border, it was built by the Henry family to cull timber from their vast holdings. J. E. Henry (father to the aforementioned Charles Henry) settled the town after building a 200-horsepower steam sawmill in the area. The family made quick work of development, a feat that included building an eleven-mile-long Zealand Valley Railroad system that crisscrossed Carroll and Bethlehem. The company town would eventually have two railroad stations: one on the Boston, Concord, and Montreal line; the other on the Portland and Ogdensburg line. Within short order, a boarding house went up, as did nicer homes for the Henry family and their managers, a store, engine house, large charcoal kilns, and post office (this operated from 1883 to 1897). A school was set up in one of the homes.

Yet within a decade, most of the saleable lumber in the Zealand Valley had been harvested or burned in forest fires. An article from *The New York Times* dated July 11, 1886, reported that "the rain of today has nearly put out the forest fires west of Fabyans (Carroll) and they are now under control. The loss is estimated at $45,000, which falls upon J. E. Henry. The smoke is clearing away."

In 1892, the Henrys purchased several thousand acres around Lincoln and moved their operations there. Another businessman, George Van Dyke, leased their mill and built the Little River Railroad along its namesake sluiceway. He operated for a few years, eking out the last vestiges of lumbering that he could. But Zealand ultimately suffered the fate of many a New England mill before and after: In 1897, it and several other buildings on the property were destroyed by fire. By then, it was essentially a moot point anyway, as timber supplies had been almost completely exhausted due to continuous logging and additional wildfires. Around that time, the Boston and Maine Railroad closed its station at Zealand, and what was left of the town was soon abandoned.

Today, near the Zealand Campground off Route 302, history aficionados can find large cellar holes, the crumbling brick foundation of the engine house, and sections of the old railroad bed.

JOHNSON/LITTLE CANADA

Two other short-lived enterprises were the adjacent mill towns of Johnson and Little Canada (part of Lincoln in present-day Franconia Notch State Park). Although the narratives of their rise and fall are similar to those told elsewhere, they offer unique glimpses of the cultural tenor of turn-of-the-century New England.

In 1905, business partners George Johnson and Henry Stebbins inked a contract with Publishers Paper Company to cut several thousand acres of prime timberland in the northern White Mountains. They also leased a sawmill and other buildings owned by the massive timber company; a two-and-a-half-mile spur line from the Boston and Maine Railroad; and a twenty-eight-ton gear steam Shay locomotive from the Lima Locomotive Works. As operations expanded, Johnson—an experienced lumberman from Monroe located on the ragged border with Vermont—recognized the need for a logging railroad to carry timber to his mills. In 1907, he incorporated just that in the way of the Gordon Pond Railroad, a six-and-a-half-mile stretch that was in operation the following year.

A fully fitted, largely self-sustaining enterprise, Johnson grew quickly. Tax invoices from Lincoln listed a large sawmill, a small mill and their respective machinery, railroad engines and cars, an engine house, a powerhouse with three boilers, a blacksmith shop, harness shop, town store, grain storage buildings, and a large horse and cattle barn. There was also a school, boarding house, and several tenements for workers and their families. Assets included millions of board feet of uncut logs and sawn lumber. Johnson successfully petitioned the Postal Service for a post office for his town—and even served as its first postmaster.

As for Johnson's workers: Seventy-eight were listed by their names, while twenty-eight so-called Polanders were identified simply by number. This was a common derogatory practice—and not just in New England; it occurred in such immigration hubs as Ellis Island. Simply put, many official recorders could not pronounce, let alone spell, Polish names, instead finding it easier to reference them as "Polanders," "Poles," and "Russians."

In the town's bustling heyday, a reporter from *The Plymouth Record* offered a perspective on everyday life with occasional human-interest blurbs. In January, for instance, a resident had a telephone installed, and "wedding bells were soon to ring again." In February, it was reported that several Johnson boys and girls would be attending town in Lincoln. And in December, a Mrs. Ginger was reported to have moved into town for the winter, and the young son of the Pichette family was described as "quite sick."

Then we come to Little Canada. In 1910, Johnson sold some acreage of hardwood trees to Edward Matson, a Pennsylvanian in the flooring business. Matson built a mill and kiln just a little way up the Gordon Pond Railroad from Johnson. He also erected homes, a boarding house, and a wagon hub factory. The name was derived from the nationality of many of his residents, of which there were thirty-two in 1911 and 1912. Although it was common to identify settlements as "Little Canada," Matson was one of the few who referred to his location that way in official documents.

In any case, both businesses flourished for a time, then petered out. Johnson and Little Canada were both all but deserted by 1916—the former because the mill burned, and most available timber had been cut; the latter purportedly because of naïve business sense. They were the second purchase for the White Mountain National Forest, which was established in 1918. The name Johnson, despite its short time in existence, stuck around for quite some time—even on local maps. Some of its buildings, including the schoolhouse, were moved to nearby Lincoln or North Woodstock.

But as we have seen time and time again, hardly anything else remains.

AND THE REST?

Lumber operations also sprouted up around the Mount Washington Valley in the way of Carrigian, Jericho, Lewisville, Wildwood, Willowdale, Witcherville, and Veazey. Additional defunct mill villages include the Gale River Settlement in Bethlehem (producing clapboards and shingles), the Kearsarge Peg Mill (producing shoe pegs and bobbins), and Peeling (the original setting of the town of Woodstock, producing spruce oil). There was also the hill-country farming settlement of Thornton Gore (northeast of Woodstock), that rode the choppy ebbs and flows of the farming tide for close to 100 years.

Today, though, most of these former communities only live on in name—and even in that regard, they are fading.

Part IV

Vermont

The woods marched in upon the town;
Reclaiming what had been their own.
—Agnes Jones Staebner

The "Green Mountain State" is the smallest, population-wise, of all the New England cluster, and as such enjoys a relatively sleepy, pastoral existence.

Still, that doesn't mean that Vermont has been immune from the typical ups and downs, booms and busts, and shifting political and religious movements and sentiments of society both past and modern.

As such, "Le Monts Verts" has its ghost towns, too.

SEVENTEEN

GLASTENBURY

Enterprising Wilds

THIS FORMER LOGGING COMMUNITY-TURNED RESORT TOWN IS located in a hilly, forested region in the state's southwest corner close to the tri-town convergence of Vermont, New York, and Massachusetts. Now part of protected forests and considered by some to be a hotbed of the paranormal—with reports over the years of a "wild man," a "dog man," and other mythical creatures, ghosts, and satanic occurrences—Glastenbury comprises more than thirty-six square miles ascending and descending a dozen 3,000-foot mountains. It and the adjoining town of Somerset are two of five unorganized towns among Vermont's 251 municipalities, meaning their population is regarded as too small to justify having a town government; Glastenbury and Somerset also share the unique distinction of being the state's only unorganized towns that were, at one time, organized.

Glastenbury was chartered in August 1761—and interestingly, by New Hampshire Governor Benning Wentworth, as Vermont wouldn't become a state for thirty more years (1791). It was in part a move by Wentworth to challenge New York state, which technically owned the area that it referred to simply as "the wilderness." The governor chartered many uninhabited areas that actually belonged to New York as a means to irk the neighbor to the southwest.

Land speculators who had purchased rights from Wentworth came to the area long before any settlers. Homesteaders—the Robinson family being one of the most prolific—began to arrive in the area in the late 1780s, and the town parceling process began in 1790. By 1791, the first Vermont census showed that Glastenbury was comprised of thirty-four residents in six families.

Still, it wasn't until 1834 that Glastenbury was officially designated an "organized" town allowing residents to elect officials and send one member to the Vermont House of Representatives. According to later catalogers, its population was seventy in 1810, but that dropped to fifty-three in 1840 and fifty-two a decade later. Zadock Thompson's 1853 *History of Vermont, Natural, Civil and Statistical* described it as "high, broken and incapable of ever being settled," and its "streams are small." By the mid-nineteenth century, its population had never amounted to yet one hundred.

North Bennington native Governor Hiland Hall, meanwhile, who was a native of North Bennington, wrote in 1859 that Glastenbury was "one of the roughest and most mountainous towns in the state, and until quite lately has been considered a pretty safe place of retreat for bears and other wild animals." Much of the land, he added, was "wholly incapable" of cultivation, yet it had abundant spruce and hemlock that was lumbered and shipped out to more populous towns.

LUMBER APLENTY

Following the Civil War, South Glastenbury grew up around brick charcoal kilns and the Bennington & Glastenbury Railroad (running, as its name would imply, between the two towns).

Its building in 1872 was considered impracticable by engineers due to the area's heavy grade and the elevation that had to be reached over a short distance. But it was commenced and completed, its tracks climbing 1,260 vertical feet over roughly eight miles. This enabled the Bennington & Glastenbury Railroad Mining & Manufacturing Company to set to work clearcutting area forests. The enterprise owned 18,000 acres across Glastenbury and surrounding townships and operated two sawmills and twelve kilns. About two million feet of lumber was produced annually.

The company also engaged in the laborious manufacture of charcoal as its use became more widespread with the thriving, post-war iron industry. The sooty by-product of wood burning was used in massive quantities to fuel blast furnaces, bloomeries, forges, and foundries producing high-quality iron. The Glastenbury area was a perfect candidate for coal making because it was remote and had thousands upon thousands of acres of trees. The Glastenbury-Woodford region became one of Vermont's foremost charcoal producers: There were at least twenty-one kilns in the area.

These were between twelve and sixteen feet high and twenty-eight to thirty feet in diameter and required a half-dozen men a day to load them with ongoing, significant cords of wood. Local kilns produced about 28,000 bushels of charcoal a month—enough to make 155 tons of iron. This was hauled out by rail; returning trains brought alcohol, mail, and other goods.

Roughly fifty men were employed in the pursuits of lumbering and charcoal production, many of them Swedish immigrants. Due to bad weather in 1873, they were only able to work about fifteen days out of every month.

In 1883, the town was described by a local gazetteer as having thirty permanent residents with several others who were "transient and therefore not enumerated." The year 1880 proved to be the height of its population at 241.

Because they were so scattered, there was no church or post office in town; residents had to attend services and receive mail in Shaftsbury and South Shaftsbury (depending on whether they lived on the north or south end of town).

The close of the 1880s, however, brought with it the end of the charcoal era as well as the logging railroad. In March 1889, the Bennington & Glastenbury Railroad Mining and Manufacturing Company ceased railroad operations.

However, an electrified railroad began running through the region to bring passengers to Camp Comfort in Woodford; this also carried day-trippers, seasonal hunters, fishermen, berry pickers, and fern-pickers. The enterprising few who came to harvest the latter abundant greenery sent their bounty to wholesale florists and meat producers in New York (who used it to display meat).

FRESH AIR—AND NEW LIFE

It seemed that the area would maintain its depopulated wilds—and then, in 1897, a handful of local businessmen got the idea to cash in on its remote, mountainous, scenic backdrop in the way of a summer resort. They set to work refashioning the sawmill and boarding-house into a hotel and clubhouse; the country store into an inn; the surrounding hillside into croquet and tennis grounds. A hatchery was also stocked with thousands of trout to attract fishermen.

The hotel was outfitted with a dining room that served oysters and clams; a hall for dancing, opera, concerts, and other events; a pool, reading room and bowling and billiards room; and an icehouse with a capacity of 130 tons. There were family apartments and twenty rooms. The property's investors made widespread structural improvements and put in new floors and ceilings, a double veranda, and fifty new windows. According to local records, these building improvements cost investors $4,590.

The Glastenbury Inn was opened the next summer to much fanfare, and in July, life was "in full midsummer swing," according to the *Troy Daily Times* and *Bennington Banner*, whose reporters were invited for a several-course trout dinner, drinks, and cigars. They described the nine-mile route by rail from Bennington offering views of the "bright, clear stream" that coursed through the valley and the forests coming down to greet it. For several miles, "there is not a human habitation in sight, nothing but vast mountains and interminable forests," according to one reporter, who also described the buzzing of the trolly a "novelty in these vast forest-clad domains."

The trolley did some "hard climbing" on the ride up, finally reaching a height of about 2,000 feet. On the return trip it was usually detached from the overhead wire and descended back to Bennington by mere gravity. Still, the rustic nature of this rail ride didn't dissuade visitors. "On every bright, warm afternoon the cars of the company are well filled with ladies, summer visitors and others, who are simply enjoying a trolley ride or who are in search of a few hours of restful quiet among the mountains," one writer marveled.

And although it was but the property's first summer in business, one reporter called it a record-breaker in terms of good-sized parties. Some came for just a day or two; others for several weeks. Visitors included politicians, the state auditor, parties of wealthy lawyers, numerous families, even a French artist who sat for three days a week on a rock in the middle of a stream to sketch the sweep of the valley.

A July 26 article in *Troy Daily Times* described it as memorable in every respect, "besides the gamy fish." The proprietors, the reporter wrote, were doing their best to make the resort attractive, and "a large and growing patronage shows that (these) efforts are being appreciated. The inn is a refreshing refuge from the heat and bustle of the village, and the ride up, one of the most picturesque possible."

Hotel owners had taken great pains to please the entourage of reporters, and it paid off. The consensus, wrote one, was that "every moment of the visit of the newspaper men was thoroughly enjoyed. The flow of good spirits was kept up from start to finish."

Such reveling, though, was short-lived. The property that had been so refurbished and appointed with luxuries maintained its grandeur for just one season. Later that year, during "the freshet of '98," floodwaters coursed freely over the clearcut forest and obliterated the railroad tracks. The resort's buildings were summarily abandoned and allowed to deteriorate (which they did over ensuing decades). What remained of the tracks was eventually dislodged and used for scrap metal.

DIMINISHING RETURNS

In the early years of the twentieth century, Glastenbury and Somerset populations were diminished to single digits. The 1920 Census recorded just seventeen in Glastenbury, the majority of these identified as boarders and transients. By the 1920s when the darkness of the Great Depression began to cloak the nation, that number was down to a paltry seven (these of the members of the Mattison and Hazard families). In nearby Somerset, twenty people—most of them of the Taylor family—were recorded in the 1930 Census.

With so few citizens in town, it was natural that family members dominated municipal offices. This might normally have gone unchecked, but the practice was of concern at a wider state level because they still held legislative seats in the state legislature. Glastenbury and Somerset, towns of barely single digits and dominated by nepotism, had vastly disproportionate power in the state capital of Montpelier. This first irritated other towns; as it continued, they became irate. In the mid-1930s, for instance, the syndicated cartoon *Believe It or Not* by Ripley published a sketch of a man and two women with the caption: "The Mattison family is the whole town of Glastenbury, Vt. Ira Mattison and his wife and his mother hold every town office."

Glastenbury and Somerset, because of their size and their distant location "in the wilds" from Montpelier, became synonymous. In 1937, public outcry against the tiny hamlets only became louder when criminal charges were brought against John H. Taylor of Somerset. He was accused of abusing his foster children. The family had already gained notoriety with their "corrupt one-family rule." As decried in one newspaper report at the time: "Taylor's wife is serving her seventh consecutive term as representative in the Legislature. . . . Somerset has a population of less than 10."

The same accusations were leveled against the Mattisons of Glastenbury, public hatred only fueled by a 1936 *Vermont Yearbook* that listed family members as selectmen, tax collectors, constables, school directors, treasurers, auditors, clerks, overseers, and school directors. Mattisons also filled the roles of road commissioner, grand juror, fire warden, health officer, and superintendent of schools.

The population in 1936? Just seven—meaning that the majority of these were double or triple posts. Making things worse, the town treasurer's ledger (we can only assume they were a Mattison, too) listed cash payments to Ira N., Aurilla and Angelia Mattison for working on town roads, for school purposes, and for bobcat bounties.

On March 26, 1937, the state had had enough: Bills were introduced in the legislature to declare the towns of Somerset and Glastenbury unorganized. They were both easily passed and the towns were disorganized. By year's end they were officially stripped of their municipality statuses, reducing the number of towns in

Vermont to 246. The Mattison family slowly died off or moved away and were all gone by 1950—leaving Glastenbury with an official population of one.

The town sat vacant and unperturbed until the 1980s, when it was slowly sold off to the United States Forest Service. The entity now owns 96 percent of the former town of Glastenbury, now the Glastenbury Wilderness in the Green Mountain National Forest. Today, the vast 26,000-acre stretch of forest is a wildlife preserve and a popular recreation spot. And, as for resident humans, it is not completely deserted: Its population was listed as nine in the 2020 Census.

A writer for the *Bennington Banner* may have put it best in an article that ran on New Year's Eve in 1977—the thirtieth anniversary of the official disincorporation of the two towns: "Their populations were almost gone, and these towns that once supported hundreds of loggers and dozens of hardscrabble farms reverted to the deer and bobcat."

A similar state by which they both exist to this day.

EIGHTEEN

BRATTLEBORO

The Perfect Community

EVERYONE WAS EQUAL, ALL MEN AND WOMEN WERE MARRIED TO one another, all property (land, homes, objects, and otherwise) belonged to anyone and everyone, and socialism and religion were intricately intertwined.

These were the teachings of John Humphrey Noyes, and they were carried out in a "utopia" that he established in the nineteenth century. A native of Brattleboro, the self-professed modern-day Moses founded a movement known as Perfectionism. This order took root in Putnam, Vermont, in the southeast sliver of the state tucked close to New Hampshire. Perfectionism was maligned by wider mainstream religions—and wider society—because it challenged contemporary social views on property ownership, gender roles, child-rearing practices, monogamous marriage, sexual practices, and work.

But it was these very values, as well as the belief that learning should be a lifelong practice, and work should be enjoyable that sustained the group for more than thirty years—making it one of the most successful and longest-lasting communal experiments of the nineteenth century.

Noyes was born in Brattleboro in 1811 to wealthy, influential and pious parents. His father was a congressman and a graduate of the Ivy League Dartmouth College. His mother Polly, sixteen years his father's senior, was religious and strong-willed. She always taught her children "to fear the Lord," and it was said that she even prayed before John Humphrey's birth that someday he might become a devoted minister of the Gospel (in a sense, those prayers were answered). But as a young man, Noyes was considered a rebel to his family; he had little interest in religion—in fact he was very cynical of it—nor a passion for theology or his educational studies, for that matter. Even so, he did well enough in his educational pursuits to get into Dartmouth, which he entered in 1826. He went on to practice law in Brattleboro while working to overcome what he called the "family affliction." That was, shyness to the point of incapacitation around women.

But at his mother's behest, he eventually attended a four-day revival in Putney, Vermont, that was presided over by Charles Grandison Finney. This was the peak of the revival movement—known as the Second Great Awakening—which was led by so-called Father of Revivalism Finney, a Connecticut native. Still, Noyes was not impressed. That was, until not long after the meeting he suffered "a feverish cold which led him to think of death, and to humble himself before God," as he described it later. It was then that he embraced faith and the idea of the Millennial Kingdom—or that a golden age of paradise would occur on earth prior to the final judgment. He went on to study at, and graduate from, Andover Newton Theology School and Yale Divinity School.

But it was while studying at Yale that he came to a new concept of the way to salvation. This did not align with the Calvinist view that, despite upwardly upholding the law, humankind possessed an inward distortion that made us unpleasing to God. He could not come to grips with the idea that he was forever a sinner, as he did not feel deep guilt or despair. Instead, Noyes posited, humans reached a state of perfection upon conversion, and were completely released of all sin. The way to salvation was reaching perfection, or at least what he considered it to be. He also believed that the second coming of Christ was not a future event, but that it had already occurred, and within just a generation of Christ's ministry on earth.

NEW, RADICAL CONCEPTS

He labeled this idea Perfectionism.

Not surprisingly, it proved to be too radical, even blasphemous, for presiding religious officials. He was denied ordination as a pastor.

Not dissuaded, Noyes continued developing his theories and traveled New England and New York for several weeks to try to attract converts. He did succeed with Abigail Merwin, falling in love with her in the process. But she left his newfound order to marry another man; that, coupled with the fact that he had been unsuccessful in garnering any followers, led to what he called a "dark night of the soul." Still, he started writing articles for a new religious periodical called the *Battle-Axe*, with his first piece denouncing the institution of marriage. And through his interpretation of biblical prophecy, he concluded that he was an agent of God.

It was around that time that his teachings attracted the attention of Harriet Holton, who came from an aristocratic family that included the then-lieutenant governor of Vermont. She began to financially support him. In 1838, he wrote her a letter: If they wed, it would be a spiritual union, and they would both benefit if they did not give in to carnal pleasures. Their marriage would advance the work of God and prove to others that he was not promoting celibacy. It would also monetarily help the movement, as her family was wealthy.

Apparently, she was convinced; later that year they were married. Noyes also arranged the marriages of his sisters to the two men who had become his closest followers, John L. Skinner and John R. Miller. He also gained the loyalty of his younger brother George, and eventually that of his traditionally pious mother.

By 1840, the movement had come into being "as a purely religious body." The self-identified prophet and his small band of followers put their complex, ever-evolving belief system into full practice at their own "Promised Land." This 500-acre commune was established in Putney, Vermont, a little way north of Brattleboro.

In 1844, the group adopted their own brand of socialism. Noyes espoused that socialism without religion was impossible and taught that an extended family system could dissolve selfishness and serve as an example of the practicality of perfectionism.

The thirty-seven members lived together in three houses and established a chapel for worship. They also ran a store and maintained two farms. In the beginning, they were supported by money willed by Noyes' father. Then slowly, they began adopting their leader's more radical teachings of "complex marriage," "male continence," "ascending fellowship," and "mutual criticism." It was these tenets, especially the first, that would ultimately lead to his notoriety. Under it, every man was married to every woman, and vice versa. Any pairing was permitted to have sexual intercourse, the only rule being that couples couldn't get attached. Also, sexual partners had to gain each other's consent, "not by private conversation and courtship, but through the intervention of some third person or persons," as stipulated by Noyes. Monogamy and exclusivity in partnership was considered selfish and idolatrous.

As he wrote in a published pamphlet: "In a holy community, there is no more reason why sexual intercourse should be restrained by law, than why eating and drinking should be—and there is as little occasion for shame in one case as in the other."

This system also involved "male continence," a method of birth control with attributes of tantric sex. In its practice, a couple would have sex without the man ejaculating either during or after the act, Noyes concluded this after his wife had given birth to four premature children who later died. Therefore, he surmised, it was a waste of his seed and was no different or better than masturbation.

Then there was the practice of "ascending fellowship." This was set up to introduce virgins into complex marriage and to prevent young members from falling exclusively in love with one another—thus limiting their ability to feel affection for anyone but other young members. Certain people, those identified as being closer to God and dubbed a "central member," presided over the commune's virgins. These special members were permitted to choose any virgin of their choice—who was required to accept. Female "central members" were typically past menopause; this allowed them to enforce in their younger lovers the concept of male continence.

Noyes' fourth major teaching, "mutual criticism," allowed members to be freely criticized by either a committee or the community at large. These critiques typically had to do with a member's bad traits, or those that "detracted from family unity." It was encouraged that they be a "shameful, humiliating experience." Noyes, not unexpectedly, was immune from the practice, justifying that it was harmful if a group criticized their leader.

Many of these values were only practiced among leadership until being fully adopted by all community members once the group had relocated to Oneida, New York.

In 1847, just seven years after settling in their paradise in Putney, the group concluded that "the kingdom of God had come"—meaning that Christ's second coming had already taken place. Also, they believed, they could bring about the millennial kingdom themselves.

But as their beliefs came to light in general society, they were reviled and criticized. As a further blow to the Perfectionist order, member Daniel Holt defected in 1847 and accused Noyes of adultery. He also revealed the group's extremist lifestyle and beliefs.

SETTLEMENT PERFECTED

Appalled and humiliated and not wanting to become a martyr, Noyes fled with "irreligious haste," as one historian put it. The group willingly followed; they believed that he was a modern-day infestation of Moses and would lead them to the promised land. They resettled on a twenty-three-acre property in Oneida, New York, northwest of Albany near Lake Ontario on the Canadian border. At the time, the order had forty-five members. By the end of 1848, their number nearly doubled to eighty-seven. At its peak in 1878, the community would comprise of 306.

The Perfectionist's economic base was largely agricultural: They grew crops on forty cleared acres. They also had a sawmill that produced lumber, and they eventually established minor craft industries. Most notably, member Charles Craigan led the creation of the now ubiquitous silver-plated flatware Oneida. This was sold under Oneida Limited, and its growing profits allowed the community to sustain itself. At the time, the silverware they manufactured was a rarity.

The group also built a large brick mansion where they could live as one family and continue practicing complex marriage. They appointed administrative committees, practiced equality among the sexes, and espoused education as a lifelong practice. For example, after work in the evenings they would sing, pray, and study Hebrew, Greek, and Latin. They held weekly services that welcomed outsiders.

One journalist who visited at the time was impressed, gushing even. "I looked in vain for the visible signs of either the suffering or the sin," he wrote. "The fact that the children of the community hardly ever wish to leave it, that the young men whom they send to Yale College, and the young women whom they send for musical instruction to New York, always returned eagerly and devote their lives to the community—this proves a good deal."

The community ultimately fell into a pattern of daily living that was observed for the next thirty years. Their ability to sustain themselves for such a long period made them one of the most successful communes of the nineteenth century.

As evidence of this, a small branch group was established in Brooklyn, Connecticut, in 1849, and others followed in Wallingford, Connecticut, Manlius, Connecticut, and Newark, New Jersey.

Still, there were schisms. Member Charles Guiteau left in 1866 after repeatedly failing to find sexual partners. He denounced the community, contending that premature sex stunted the growth of female members and also made them homely and emaciated. Not helping the situation, fifteen years later he would assassinate President James A. Garfield on July 2, 1881. A loyal Republican, he was convinced that his work for the Republican Party had been critical to Garfield's election and was paranoid that the President would destroy the party by eliminating the patronage system. Removing him, Guiteau believed, would elevate Vermont native Chester A. Arthur and prevent Garfield from doing any damage. Guiteau was later identified as having a narcissistic personality.

The Perfectionist movement was further imperiled when Noyes put his son, Ted, in charge. A doctor and an agnostic, he was an authoritarian who was soon resented by the people of Oneida. Factions arose. Added to that, there was growing hostility and opposition from the surrounding community. This prompted the elder

Noyes to drop the system of complex marriage. Many members quickly married.

Still, it wasn't enough. The community couldn't recover or re-unify. In January 1881, the commune was abandoned. Noyes and a few followers moved to Canada. Noyes died there in 1886. A few other remaining members established a joint stock company, Oneida Community, Ltd., which continued their various industry, most notably silverware. It was later acquired, and the Oneida brand continues to be sold through the Oneida Group. The company, according to its website, strives for perfection "like the community that created it."

The former Perfectionist enclave is now the Oneida Community Mansion House, a nonprofit museum. The 93,000-square-foot building is designated as a National Historic landmark. It features period rooms that have been preserved or restaged, as well as permanent, changing, and interpretive exhibits. The building's large-scale interior layout represents the changing architectural styles and innovations of the 1800s (it was built over four phases) and is "a testament to the Community's core beliefs about communal life," as described by the nonprofit that manages it.

Interestingly, the values that sustained the community and were denigrated and reviled at the time—notably socialism and equality of the sexes—are held up today as forward-thinking. This is evidenced in a proclamation by the Mansion House's overseeing committee. Their mission is "to share the story of the Oneida Community—one of the most radical and successful of the 19th century social experiments—to explore pressing social issues that still confront audiences today."

NINETEEN

INDUSTRIOUS HILLS

As was the case with other New England states, Vermont's green hills were mined and milled throughout the eighteenth and nineteenth centuries. But what differentiates the Green Mountain State from its neighbors is its rich deposits of slate and copper.

One of the foremost sites for the latter—and also a notorious blotch on rural Vermont history when floundering mill profits fomented a protest that was elevated by the press to a "war"— was the fittingly named Coppertown (later Ely Copper Mines). Located in Vershire in east-central Vermont close to the New Hampshire border and its expansive White Mountains, the mines sat atop a vein of copperas, or iron sulfur, that stretches up the Appalachian Mountain chain from Georgia to Maine.

The deposit had numerous industrial applications in early nineteenth century tanning and textile industries. More significantly, early mine operators quickly realized that they could extract valuable copper from it. Vermont was foremost in the country when it came to copper production: At their peak, state mines were yielding 60 percent of the overall U.S. market.

The Vermont Copper Mining Co. opened the mine in Vershire in 1854. It was the only mine in the state to smelt copper on a large scale (rather than shipping it elsewhere for processing).

Shortly thereafter, Smith Ely, an heir to a New Jersey leather manufacturing company and an original shareholder, won an election to become company president. He would eventually own about 90 percent of the mine.

Initially, it was a good bet on his part, as the production and prices of copper increased in the 1870s. To meet demand, the company expanded its smelting plant; this soon stretched 700 feet and encompassed twenty-four furnaces. Sections of the mine were also extended to a depth of 1,000 feet. At this time, the workforce was around 700, comprised of many immigrants from Ireland and Cornwall, England. The latter had some of the richest tin and copper deposits in the British Isles and was known for its long tradition of skilled labor.

By 1880, the town population grew to 1,875. The town of Copperfield itself accelerated right along with it. There was a Methodist church and Catholic church, numerous schools, a post office, meat market, livery, and meeting hall that served as both a hotel and the company store. There was also a barbershop, and even a women's hat shop. Most of the workers lived in company housing, and because Copperfield was a dry town, they often went elsewhere for drinks and entertainment.

But it was a hard living. Miners suffered injuries on the job and also contracted typhus from unclean drinking and bathing water (the result of pollution from mines and poorly located privies). There was also the ever-pervasive pungent stench of sulfur that hung over the village.

In 1876 as he was getting up in years, Smith Ely brought his grandson, the redundantly named Ely Ely-Goddard, into the family business as a successor. But the young man quickly fell out of favor with the miners: He built an elegant mansion, Elysium, that held dominion over the otherwise humble shacks and dingy smelter. He became notorious for his ostentatious clothing, handsome horses and coaches, and lively parties—this all-in contrast to the workers toiling away and barely eking out livings. Furthermore, in 1879, after being elected to the legislature, he successfully pushed through a petition to change the town name to Ely. Three years later, townspeople—reflecting their displeasure and portending things to come—successfully petitioned to change it back to Vershire.

But in the typical boom-and-bust nature of industry, by the 1880s, the Vermont Copper Mining Co. was floundering. The mine was producing less copper because of a diminished supply, and prices were concurrently falling. This was due in part to the fact that native copper—or that which didn't have to be extracted through roasting and smelting—was discovered in Michigan and other points west. As a cost-cutting measure, employees were fired—yet, at the same time, the company expended purportedly dwindling funds on blast furnaces and pneumatic drills. This investment proved frivolous; the company fell further into debt.

THE "VERSHIRE WAR"

As such, it neglected its workers: By July 1883, miners had gone without paychecks for at least two months. Company executives claimed that the mine was nearly bankrupt and informed workers that, if they wanted to keep their jobs, they would have to take a sizable pay cut. Understandably on the part of workers, it seemed all but impossible that their employer would claim to be bereft of funds when just years prior the consumer price of copper was at an all-time high and business was thriving. The roughly 300 miners still employed demanded that their back wages be paid immediately.

The demand was not met.

Fed-up, workers acted. On Monday, July 2, they stormed the company store (without money, they had not been able to afford food or other goods). Then they moved in on Ely-Goddard's mansion. When they found he wasn't home, they descended on the nearby town of West Fairlee, where the elderly, infirm Smith Ely was staying. The incensed crowd was somehow persuaded to form a committee to meet with Smith. Later news reports portrayed him as sympathetic to the rioters: He was quoted as saying, "This mine belongs to the working man." Other conflicting reports said he got out of bed to meet them and explained that he was doing all he could to raise the money that the company owed them.

Accounts of the events between July 2 and July 8 were published widely. Locally, the *Green Mountain Freeman* called it the "Vershire Affair," describing a "crowd of ignorant men goaded by ill usage and hunger" ultimately a type of assembly that was "apt to be a very willing tool in the hands of the first communistic agitator that comes along."

The *Burlington Free Press*, meanwhile, ramped up the rhetoric by calling it the "Vershire War." One reporter called the town "wofully (sic) shabby," Ely-Goddard's Elysium "vulgar looking beyond belief," and the smelter "hideous" with a "beastly" odor. All told, the stripped and mined town was "the most utterly God-forsaken in the whole world." Still, the reporter maintained sympathy for the miners, calling them "poor benighted souls whose wrongs had urged them into frenzy."

At mid-week, after days of rioting, mine counsel Roswell Farnham arrived to offer miners one-fifth of what they were owed—and this with the condition that they continue to process the remaining copper so that it could be sold off.

Not surprisingly, they refused.

Instead, according to eyewitness accounts, they stole a wagon, drove it to the house of the mine manager, and pilfered his possessions (the manager had fled town when hearing of the protests). They also purportedly kidnapped several West Fairlee businessmen, brought them to the mine and told them to tell the men to find some way to pay them. The "hostages" were released shortly thereafter. But that didn't mean that the insurrection was over: Workers seized explosives and threatened more significant damage than had already been levied if they were not duly paid.

That escalation prompted townspeople and the local sheriff—who had stayed within the shelter of their homes for several days—to appeal to Governor John Barstow. He immediately called in four companies of militia. On the morning of Saturday, July 7, five days into the standoff, roughly 200 soldiers rode to the outskirts of town. They were provided with ample ammunition.

A report in the July 13, 1883, edition of the *Burlington Free Press* described the overall sentiment as they marched on the town. "Here, in the street of a quiet Vermont village, in a time of profound peace the country over, marched four companies of Vermont soldiers, armed not against foreign foe but against our own people and ready if necessary to shoot them down."

But as they came into Vershire at dawn—when most inhabitants, miners included, were sleeping—no one was in sight. Moving into the town, they were met with silence and tentative curtain pulls. Eventually townspeople wandered out to meet them. The miners, once located, surrendered. Twelve of them identified as the lead culprits were arrested and taken off to jail—but with no serious property damage ensuing, and no one willing to testify against them, they were released shortly thereafter.

Soldiers took pity. The "crazed mob" they had expected was nothing more than a group of hungry miners and their families.

They shared rations of cheese, crackers, and canned beef, according to later accounts.

Several hours after they had arrived expecting bloodshed, the militia departed. No one was injured, and no shots were fired.

The miners were eventually paid some of what they were owed—but not all of it. They and their families soon began an exodus, heading elsewhere in search of work. The company, not wanting to cut its losses even despite the "affair" or "war," held on for a few years. But executives eventually declared bankruptcy and, with the dawn of the twentieth century, the mine was purchased by businessman George Westinghouse. It was briefly the site of smelting experiments; but by 1907 Westinghouse gave up on that venture and auctioned off its buildings and equipment.

Houses were also disassembled and stripped; the massive stones and boulders underpinning the mines removed. The Methodist church was moved to South Vershire, then Vershire, where it now serves as a community building. The Catholic church was relocated to West Fairlee. A farmer bought the once-grand Elysium for $150 and had it transported to a hillside overlooking West Fairlee.

Coppertown or Ely—however those who lived there or near it choose to remember it—was no more.

It sat abandoned and polluted with hundreds of thousands of cubic yardage of waste rock, slag heap, and ore beds, not to mention thousands of feet of dangerous, deteriorated underground tunnels. In 2001, the Environmental Protection Agency (EPA) finally stepped in and declared it a Superfund site. The designation is given to locales that have been contaminated by hazardous waste, typically from mining sites, manufacturing facilities, and processing plants.

As of 2019, the EPA reported that the cleanup of the Ely mines would cost $24 million. In the end, as is often the case, the land was left to suffer from human mistake and mistreatment.

WEST CASTLETON

Another industry in which Vermont was a standout was slate.

In fact, at its peak, the production of slate in Vermont was only topped by that of Pennsylvania.

The state has three significant slate belts yielding slate in shades of red, purple, and two different shades of green. The belt stretching across mid-western Vermont into New York contains the most diverse colors, notably purple and green—and thus greater possibilities in terms of profits.

In the mid-1800s, rail construction opened up new markets for Vermont's high-quality slate deposits. The West Castleton Railroad and Slate Company capitalized on this, setting up operations at a 600-acre parcel tucked between Glen Lake and the much larger Lake Bomoseen. It is believed to have been the state's only slate company at the time. The area was a known slate locale and had previously been settled by experienced quarrymen from Wales, Ireland, France, and Slavic nations. In short order, the area was cluttered with twenty-five quarries employing 800 workers.

Business was profitable from the start, as slate was in demand for roofing tiles, fireplace mantles, billiard tables, blackboards, and sometimes foundations and steps. As noted by *The People's Journal* in April 1854: "The constantly increasing demand for slate from these quarries bids fair to render them, if they are not now, one of the principal sources of wealth in Vermont."

In 1853, several quarries and sawmills were in operation in West Castleton, and the village comprised of forty-three houses, a school, and a store. As was the presiding practice in mining, milling, and logging towns, the company owned all the housing, sold all its food and clothing, and controlled transportation. Workers, who put in ten-hour days and earned less than $2 an hour for their arduous labors, were expected to shop at the company store. During times of currency shortages—such as was the case amidst the Civil War—they were issued a form of bank credit known as scrip.

All mining, by its very nature, is difficult and dangerous—and slate even more so. Its quarrying requires blasting, manual labor, and teams of animals, and 85 percent of the material unwillingly dislodged from the earth is wasted. Many workers were killed in blasting accidents, or by collapsing rock. After slate was laboriously extracted from West Castleton, it was hauled to a wharf on Bomoseen, loaded into cars and ferried to the railroad in nearby Hydenville.

Concurrently with the demand for high-quality slate was a growing market for marbleized slate—this involved a process that made inexpensive slate resemble marble. It allowed the middle class to possess similar symbols of wealth as their genteel neighbors; it was especially popular in mantles.

By 1855, the West Castleton Company had built a $2,000 kiln on the west shore of Bomoseen that was used to marbleize slate. In 1868, the company also built a mill to prepare purple and green flooring, billiard tables, and sinks and washtubs. At the time it was constructed, it was one of the country's largest finishing mills, powered by a twenty-four-foot waterwheel, and containing circular saws, a band saw and jigsaw, planers, rubbing beds, and a jointer. After the mill burned in 1870, it was rebuilt on a smaller scale.

Slate quarrying continued to be profitable up until the start of the Great Depression. A decline in the demand for roofing slate, coupled with nearly exhausted quarries, led to the closing of the Lake Shore-West Castleton mill in 1929.

Today, the site sits within the confines of Bomoseen State Park, which stretches across the towns of Castleton, Fair Haven, Hubbardton, and Benson. Its last vestiges can be viewed along the reserve's Slate History Trail. A self-guided walking tour takes visitors past the final deteriorating remnant of the slate mill; piles of slate rubble; foundations of former workers' homes; and the old mill, dam, and quarry. At the quarry, there are also double stacks of slate known as "dead men" that anchored derricks and pulleys used to hoist slate blocks.

As for the slate itself, much of it was shipped off for use in other areas of the country, but it can be seen around the Fair Haven and Poultney areas—as well as over the border in New York—lining roofs and sidewalks. Some tombstones have even been fashioned from the uniquely colorful material—a fitting memoriam for an industry that for nearly eighty years served as the area's lifeblood.

LITTLE RIVER/RICKER BASIN

Chiseled into the side of a granite-studded hill in Waterbury, Little River (also known as Ricker Basin or Ricker Mountain) was a busy mill town and farming community that existed for more than a century.

In the early 1800s, the industrial-minded Joseph Ricker purchased the parcel of land—in the north-central part of the state as it widens to an elongated triangle—that would eventually bear his name. He soon set to the arduous work of clearing it; trees were felled and stumps and large boulders were hauled away by teams of horses and oxen.

With the Little River as one of its primary geographic features, the town sat at the base of Ricker Mountain, and when it was active, covered about 4,000 acres. When the railroad finally made its way to Waterbury by mid-century, the farming community began to flourish. At its most peopled, it was estimated to be home to fifty families and three thrumming sawmills that took advantage of plentiful wood supplies and water access. The village also hosted a church, several businesses, five schools and two cemeteries—not to mention numerous farms dotting its hills.

The town was largely self-sufficient, and residents were mostly subsistence farmers who struggled to grow crops on rocky soil and mountain terrain that is notoriously challenging to till. They also raised and slaughtered livestock and produced maple syrup, sugar, and soap.

But as the years progressed (and families didn't), residents began to move away, abandoning homes and land. Many members of the younger generation, who weren't interested in pursuing the family livelihood, were beckoned by larger towns and cities and flatter land to the west. By the late 1800s, the town population had considerably dwindled.

There was a brief period of renewed prosperity from 1916 to 1922; the Waterbury Last Block Co. sawmill manufactured gunstocks and ammunition at the end of World War I. Though it only lasted a little over half a decade, at one time it had thirty-five men working along with forty-four teams of horses. The notorious floods of 1927 and 1934 prompted many families to pull up stakes. The Ricker Basin community was cut off, and in surrounding towns, the waters rose so high that people had to be rescued from the tops of roofs where they had sought refuge. It was reported that there were fifty-five casualties.

As was the case elsewhere in New England, these ravaging storms were the impetus for the Waterbury Dam and reservoir, which ultimately submerged the paltry remains of the Ricker Basin community.

Today, what is left of the old village has been preserved as part of Little River State Park (north of the dam that required its final washing out). Compared to other abandoned towns where not even traces remain, it seems a treasure trove: One farmhouse owned by

Almeron Goodell remains intact, as well as a cemetery, numerous structural foundations, and remnants of machinery.

The nearly 150-year-old Goodell house stands, albeit unsteadied by the years, atop a little rise nearly obscured by birch trees and ferns. A crude, barely legible sign held in place by two rusted nails on its edifice announces: "A Goodell Farm/Only House Still Standing in Ricker Basin." It is a humble two-story box, clapboards blackened by time and the elements, moss and lichen clinging to the uneven shingles on its roof, brick chimney tilted and crumbled. Modern-day vandals have made their presence known: The front door has been partly bashed in, some windows have been boarded up, and graffiti serves as a sort of crude wallpaper. Otherwise, its interior is bare and bereft of belongings, save for an old rusted and handicapped cast iron stove, what look to be deteriorating washtubs, and a couple of benches.

No doubt its namesake Almeron was once proud of the structure he had built: He purchased his small subsistence farm in Ricker Basin in 1863. He then spent most of his adult life on the farm, building the house frame using rough-hewn timbers and splitting its roof shingles by hand. According to a plaque at the site, in 1870 he had four cows, one horse and a flock of chickens, which was enough to supply his family's needs. When he died in 1910, he was buried in the old Waterbury Center Cemetery.

Just up the road from the Almeron homestead is a thirty-foot-by-thirty-foot family cemetery with fifteen plots marking the final resting places of generations of the Ricker family. The small burial ground is encircled with white cedars, planted by the family to honor their loved ones. Not natural to the area, these are meant to symbolically give life to the deceased. And, in a sense, they give eternal life to the deceased town, too.

LEWISTON

This once-flourishing town was located in Windsor County, flush against the New Hampshire border on the west bank of the Connecticut River.

Settlers first arrived in 1765, early among them town namesake Dr. Joseph Lewis and his family. In 1793, Lewis purchased a gristmill and sawmill on Blood Brook, which flowed eastward to the Connecticut River. More industry followed: Burton's sawmill in 1800, then a bark mill and a tannery with an attendant shoemaker. Dr. Lewis eventually ran a ferry across the river to Hanover, and a covered toll bridge was built in town in 1796. This stood for nearly 140 years until a steel-and-concrete structure took its place (decades before measures were put in place to protect historic covered bridges from such demolition).

In 1848, the town received a further boon when the Passumpsic and Connecticut Railroad laid its tracks through the village. It was the first line to service the area, and the railroad company also built a freight depot. The Boston & Maine Railroad took over operations in the 1880s, building a larger depot that still stands today. Various goods, notably coal, began flowing into the area through Lewiston.

Dartmouth College, in Hanover, New Hampshire, just across the river, heated its buildings with a central steam plant, making bituminous coal essential. In its first year, the plant consumed 1,375 tons of coal; by 1906 it was using 3,200 tons a year (or eighteen tons a day in the coldest depths of winter). This heating material had to come in through Lewiston—creating a beneficial symbiosis between the college and the town. The station also supported dairy farmers, who shipped their products out on milk trains, and transported millworkers to and from downriver White River Junction.

In the late nineteenth and early twentieth centuries, Lewiston was teeming with activity: It had a creamery, several coal yards, a sawmill, blacksmith shop, and combination general store and post office. The town also showed its salacious side during Prohibition in the 1920s when it was host to a speakeasy named, morbidly, Buckets of Blood (this was actually reference to Blood Brook). A brothel was also located a little way away from the town center (it was prohibited from the middle of town).

But by the 1920s, Lewiston's status was fading. With oil beginning to replace coal and the economy regionalizing, defunct mills were closing. Within a decade—by the early 1930s—they were all gone, and the main depot for Hanover and the college shifted to White River Junction. Lewiston's location also contributed to its demise: Although it was on the river and benefitted from that proximity, it was hemmed in on the other side by a ridge. There was little room for expansion. Post-World War II, it was becoming a bedroom community for Hanover and Norwich; landlords were converting existing homes into apartments, which benefitted them economically while also creating more housing stock.

A further detriment came in the 1950s in the way of the building of the Windsor Dam downstream. This wiped out low-lying farmland. With the town barely hanging on, the post office closed in 1954, the rail station in 1960. The final blow came in 1967 with a road-widening project to create a feeder for Interstate 91. Bulldozers demolished most of Lewiston's remaining buildings, including several warehouses and stores.

By the late 1980s, nearly two-and-a-quarter centuries after its founding, Lewiston had been diminished to a half-dozen buildings. It was acquired by Dartmouth in 1989 as part of the college's purchase of the old Hanover hospital. So ultimately, the town that had reinvented itself over its successful, 125-year run once again found new, purposeful life.

PART V

CONNECTICUT

Hello—out—there! Hello—out there!
—WILLIAM SAROYAN

Connecticut is unique and wildly diverse in many respects—history, culture, geography, landscape, population.

A state of many nicknames—"The Nutmeg State," "The Constitution State," "The Provisions State," "The Blue Law State," "The State of Steady Habits"—it made significant contributions to industry during the Revolutionary and Civil wars. Its prestigious Yale University is world-renowned. Its seafaring is unrivaled, its Mystic Seaport Museum is the largest of its kind in the United States.

Given all this, it is only fitting that Connecticut encompasses unparalleled, intriguing ghost towns, from industrial villages that have remained intact more than 100 years on; to beachside enclaves that intrigue in their decay; to hauntingly sacred former theme parts.

TWENTY

JOHNSONVILLE

The Past Revealed

It was like walking through a silent, staged movie set.

Roughly a dozen buildings encircled a central road, overlooked a tranquil pond, or clustered around a small spillway. These included houses with subtle architectural flourishes, a barn with decorative detailing, a small steepled church, a one-room schoolhouse, a humble mill with an attached waterwheel flanked by tumbledown sheds and outbuildings.

But not a person was around. The road was empty. The buildings sat hushed and empty, their only inhabitants the ghosts of the past.

Abandoned as it was, though, the town had clearly been spared the full ferocious might of the elements. No demolition crews had descended to level it. Greenery had been kept back from encroachment. Structures were sound, if marred in places cosmetically.

Until its purchase in 2017, the village of Johnsonville fulfilled the oxymoron of being one of New England's most "intact" ghost towns. Like the quintessential variety of the Old West, its buildings were relatively upkept, its central road still passable by car.

Sitting on sixty-two acres in East Haddam in the southern part of the state, Johnsonville was once a successful mill town. It was a center of twine production from the mid-1800s to the early 1920s, in fact. Later, it was envisioned as a Victorian-era tourist attraction. Then, for decades, it sat abandoned and in limbo as project after project proposed for it fell through, and it cycled on and off the market, its price decreasing with each go-around.

While the exact date of the town's settlement is unclear, by 1832 it was host to the Neptune Mill. Constructed by the Card Company and located beside an existing dam, this harnessed the power of the Moodus and Salmon rivers. The mill was one of twelve dotting the rivers' shorelines in the middle of the nineteenth century. Using new, innovative cord wrapping machines, the Neptune enterprise was able to produce twine on a massive scale—this was used primarily in fishing nets, and was distributed up and down the northeastern seaboard, to the Great Lakes, and as far as the west coast.

The mill continued expanding until it reached three stories and spanned 100 feet by 100 feet. Architecturally, it resembled a church, complete with a steeple and bell that was used to call workers to the factory every morning. A community quickly grew up around the booming operation—several homes, a church, school, store, and post office.

In 1862, thirty years after the building of the original mill, town namesake Emory Johnson erected a second mill that he named Triton. This was to either correlate it with the original mill or to ascend it—as Neptune is the Roman god of freshwater and the sea, and Triton is the Greek equivalent.

Operations thrummed along for several decades, even as the mills went through a few iterations and suffered structural damage from fires. Not much is chronicled of daily life or mill activity, however, and it remains unclear how many people lived in Johnsonville at its peak.

Despite a precipitous drop-off in demand and an ensuing dwindling population, the Neptune kept churning out product until the 1970s—making it one of the country's oldest twine mills in continuous operation at the time.

CYCLES, BUT NO CHANGE

The Johnson family continued to own the property until 1965, when eccentric businessman Raymond Schmitt stepped in. A self-made millionaire who owned aerospace equipment manufacturer AGC Corporation, Schmitt purchased the property with plans to transform it into a tourist attraction. The Neptune mill was to become the center of what he envisioned as Historic Johnsonville Village. To realize this, he began assembling a sort of full-scale dollhouse, purchasing buildings from around the east coast and transporting them to Johnsonville. These included a general store, a clock and toy store, a school, a church, a Victorian stable, and a sawmill from nearby Lyme (one of just two that had operated in Connecticut). He assembled other accoutrements, as well, including period sleighs, trolleys, streetlights, antiques, and furniture.

In 1966, he also purchased an old-fashioned steamboat at an auctioning off of items from Freedomland U.S.A. The Bronx theme park dedicated to American history had operated for just four years and was going out of business. Schmitt had the boat transported by truck to Moodus—where it sat docked in the Johnson millpond for more than thirty years.

But Schmitt's plans were stymied in 1972, when the Neptune mill was struck by lightning and burned to the ground. This was a common occurrence throughout New England history; wood frame construction and flammable machinery made them especially susceptible to conflagration.

Just like that, the historic mill attraction was without its centerpiece. Schmitt seemed to lose interest, although he, and then his family, held onto the property for another roughly thirty years. The millionaire was further dissuaded in the 1990s, when he had a zoning disagreement with the town of East Haddam. Officials had asked him to apply for a permit to put in a large pond.

Still, he rented out the town and its buildings for weddings and held occasional events. In 1988, for instance, *The New York Times* ran an ad inviting people to "celebrate Johnsonville's history and recreation with the Schmitts" at a one-day "Festival of the Forgotten Arts."

The former mill town had its moments of fame, too: Billy Joel filmed part of his *River of Dreams* music video in the village in 1993. It was also used as a backdrop for "Freedom," the 2014 film starring Cuba Gooding Jr., as well as *Deep in the Darkness*, also released in 2014 and centered around a small, creepy town that held a dark secret.

Schmitt put the property up for sale not long after the zoning disagreement. When he died in 1998, his estate auctioned off his expansive collection of antiques and other artifacts, including items—and even buildings—that he intended to use in his defunct historic theme park.

The Schmitt family was finally divested of the property in 2001, when Meyer Jabara Hotels of Danbury, Connecticut, purchased it with the intent to build a mixed-use development. The company filed plans to establish an age-restrictive, mixed-use development including thirty-three upscale single-family townhouses built in a Victorian style. But the project was scrapped due to concerns about available sewage capacity and the density of its housing component.

It was listed on the market a handful of times over the next few years, with Meyer Jabara slashing the asking price by hundreds of thousands of dollars each time so as to unload it. In October 2014, it was put up for online auction; the winning bid was $1.9 million. But after several months of haggling, the deal fell through. Others, from entrepreneurs to mediums to casino owners, expressed interested in it, but nothing ultimately materialized.

By this point, the town had begun falling into disrepair. Its on-again, off-again relationship with the real estate market was chronicled by the local press; this was then picked up by wider news outlets, then finally by the National Geographic TV series *Abandoned*. Such exposure drew interest from history lovers, paranormal researchers, ghost hunters, mediums, and the overall curiously minded. The property was private, but they descended on its outskirts to take photos and videos and collect fodder for blog posts.

There was trespassing too, of course; fearing vandalism and other damage, Meyer Jabara hired a security guard to move onto the property. The owning company also had a longtime caretaker who helped to keep the prying public in check.

The "odd little ghost town," as some called it, was listed once again in 2017, this time attracting a much wider audience because of its nationwide exposure. The real estate agent facilitating the sale told reporters that she received nearly 100 calls from prospective buyers. One finally did come through: The Philippine-based independent Christian church Iglesia ni Cristo (INC), which purchased it on July 7, 2017, for $1.85 million. On the day church officials signed the closing papers, they invited 500 members to celebrate and tour the property. Press pictures from the event depict their entourage clad in suits and other formal attire—an interesting contrast to the bucolic setting and neglected buildings.

Founded in 1913, INC has worked to expand its U.S. footprint and real estate portfolio. The Church of Christ has shown particular interest in large tracts of abandoned property, having also purchased the unincorporated community of Scenic, South Dakota, for roughly $800,000 in 2014. The entity has shared its plans to renovate Johnsonville's buildings and use them for worship spaces and recreation and sports areas for its members.

ALL THAT REMAINS

For so many decades after its industrial apex, the town has sat in a relatively untouched statis, an eerie set piece of a bygone era. The phrase is overused, but in this case, it is on point: Johnsonville is truly a town frozen in time.

But that is what has made it so fascinating. It has been identified as a ghost town for nearly as long as it was not; that moniker will stay with it no matter what comes next.

Those who have had the privilege to walk through it or peek through its gates and fences emblazoned with "No Trespassing" and "Village Closed to the Public" signs have been witness to a tangible, full-scale time capsule.

A decorative wooden sign still marks the town's entrance: "Since 1832/Neptune Twine and Cord Mills." (Although for so many years, there were no longer any visitors to greet.) Lampposts missing large strips of paint stand sentinel along the road beyond. Front and back lawns are demarcated by uneven picket fences whose whitewash coating has in turn been whitewashed by the elements.

The Emory Johnson homestead maintains its central location. Built in 1846 by the son-in-law of one of the original mill owners, the white-clapboarded, black-shuttered house with a pillared wraparound porch has four bedrooms, a solarium, three fireplaces, and numerous other Victorian-era details. Its ell stretches out in multi-leveled, multi-shaped sections. The house has been described as the gem of the property.

Other houses around it represent the shifting architectural styles of the eighteenth century: an 1846 Colonial-style dwelling; a circa-1900 one-and-a-half story residence; a two-story abode built around 1800.

Further along is the one-room Hyde School, an original schoolhouse once used by the community of East Haddam. Peering inside through its windows, one could see its rows of dust-covered desks awaiting pupils who would never return.

Nearby is the Gilead chapel, a tiny gray steepled structure that seats roughly seventy-five. Schmitt had it relocated from nearby Waterford.

The Gilbert Livery Stable is by far the decorative standout—it is believed to have been built in Winsted in 1920 (and like the chapel, moved from there by Schmitt). The commanding three-story, pale-yellow structure features peaked decorative gables and a weather-topped cupola. Inside, it was outfitted with oak stalls, beadboard, and raised paneling.

Elsewhere there is an 1899 office overlooking the fifteen-acre Johnson millpond. A meeting house, turned clock and toy store, from the 1800s. A quaint little general store with a sign designating it as such and a wrap-around porch (built in 1845 and transported from Peru, Massachusetts). A covered bridge. A small mill and waterwheel.

Relatively preserved as it has been, though—compared to other New England ghost towns where barely-there remnants can't even maintain a hold—a closer look reveals the greening stains of mildew, moss-clung shingles, weather-wearied clapboards and gables, errant vines, lilts, and sags.

So, in that sense, Johnsonville hints at its present while fully realizing its past.

TWENTY-ONE

HISTORICAL INDUSTRY

OVER THE CENTURIES, CONNECTICUT HAS PROVED THAT, WHILE it may be small in size, it has been (industrially) mighty.

GAY CITY/FACTORY HOLLOW

It is a pattern that has been repeated throughout time: Gay City (or Factory Hollow) came about as the result of religious differences. Notably, in 1796, Elijah Andrus and John Gay led a small flock of devout followers southeast from Hartford into a valley in the wilderness near Hebron.

The group was Methodist, whereas Hartford was inclined to stricter Congregationalism. Not much else is known about their exact beliefs and daily practices—only that they eschewed other religions and society in general. Colonists were not sociable and mingled very little with inhabitants of nearby settlements; they wanted to be unperturbed in their religious inclinations, daily lives, and industry. At some point, Andrus left the group (the reason why isn't clear), and Gay was appointed president of the colony, while Reverend Henry P. Sumner became its religious leader. He was a Renaissance man in every respect—not only a preacher, but a farmer, manufacturer, and financier.

The Gays soon comprised the majority of the twenty-five or more families living in the community. To support themselves, they built a sawmill along the Black Ledge River and erected homes from the lumber. Other mills followed, most notably a woolen mill that first operated under the name of William Strong and Company. Building it was quite an undertaking: Stones weighing a ton or more were dragged to the site by ox-drawn sledges.

Perhaps because they were a religious sect and more inclined to see portends, it was reported later that water unnaturally seemed to flow uphill toward the factory (a sign, some have contended, that the town was cursed). Superstitious workers, in fact, refused to go about their duties, and one apparently quit on the spot, attributing the unnatural flow to dark forces. As Agnes Jones Staebner wrote in her early nineteenth century poem "Gay City":

> *They say a hundred years ago;*
> *A laborer cried his luck was ill;*
> *Saying "It's Devil's work I know;*
> *To make free water run uphill."*

Even so, the mill provided a much-needed economic stimulus to Gay City—community leaders had recognized the ready market for cloth in Hartford and other nearby towns and cities. The town grew, more houses were built, and, as the *Hartford Courant* put it: "Gay City took on the appearance of a thriving village filled with perspiring men and newly hewn timber."

But it wasn't immune to shifting economic tides—or the consequences of war. The prospering mill failed during the War of 1812, largely due to the British blockade of New London. After the close of the de facto second Revolution, the Sumner family purchased the mill and operated under the Lafayette Manufacturing

Company. Gay City subsisted for a time on its output until the mill burned down in 1830. While it was subsequently rebuilt, Gay City never fully recovered: Prior to the long-looming Civil War, waves of exoduses occurred as people moved away to seek out factory jobs in urban hubs. The last members of the Gay family left around the 1860s. A decade later, in 1879, the rebuilt mill burned all the way to its massive stone foundations.

The last Sumner born in town was John Sumner; his son George would go on to become lieutenant governor of Connecticut, serving from 1883 to 1885. Truman Porter, for his part, was the last man to make his home in Gay City. When he died, it was deserted for good.

The property was then acquired by Emma P. Foster and her sister, Alice, descendants of the Gay family. When they died in the 1940s, they left the land to the state by will, stipulating that it be called Gay City State Park, and that whatever remained of town structures and graveyard not be purposely torn down.

Today, that park spans more than 1,500 acres across Hebron and Bolton. Gay City has left mere fragments: A warren of falling-down walls and other stone ridges that were once likely edifices; channels; a stone finger of a chimney sticking up incongruously amidst stands of narrow trees; a burial ground formed by a narrow rectangle of rock that is eerily empty except for three blanched headstones.

As Staebner lamented in her poem:

> *But this faint pathway, once a street;*
> *Is now a hushed and silent link;*
> *Whose only traffic is the feet;*
> *Of deer, come down at dusk to drink . . .*
> *The woods closed in on each redoubt;*

Shoulder to shoulder with the sun;
When the last candle flickered out;
The town was lost—the woods had won.

MINE HILL /CHALYBES/ROXBURY

This town bearing different names with the flow of centuries had a short-lived boom in the late 1860s. Located on Mine Hill and now part of a land trust in Roxbury, it was initially referred to as Chalybes. This is in reference to ancient people who lived along the Black Sea and were known to the Greeks and Romans as pioneers of ironmaking. Their Greek name translates to "tempered iron, steel."

The area first drew notice for its rich granite deposits after Yale University professor Benjamin Silliman visited in 1817; he was impressed by the stone of "light, agreeable gray" that he came across, declaring it "singularly perfect." It's not clear exactly when quarrying first began, but historians say the first granite was most likely cut by locals on an informal basis before 1850.

In 1865, workers constructed a maze of iron mines, a blast furnace and steeling puddling furnace, two roasting ovens, and a rolling mill along a ridge of the Shepaug River in what came to be known as Chalybes. The first load of ore came in January 1867. The site was soon bustling, drawing hundreds of miners, stone cutters, masons, and other laborers. The town grew with demand—a gristmill, creamery, lumber yard, general store, boarding house, hotel, and tavern soon went up. There was also a cigar shop, a hattery, even a brothel. More than 200 workers were employed in various capacities at the mine, which shipped the large slabs it quarried to Bridgeport by rail; these were then transferred by barge to New York City.

The mill was one of eight that operated in the area over two centuries, and at its peak, it smelted ten tons of iron a day. The strong and "perfect" granite that it yielded was used in foundations, door-steps, chimneys, walkways, hearths, chimneys, and other structures. It was even used in the buttresses of New York City's 59th Street Bridge and in the railroad approach to Grand Central Terminal.

But success was short-lived. The furnace was shut down and production ceased in 1868, two critical factors contributing to its downfall: It employed production techniques that were a decade behind the times, and it began to compete with the vast reserves of iron ore that were opening up in the West. The steel mill was dismantled and moved to Bridgeport.

It was left to the whims of Mother Nature, who struck her final fury with the Hurricane of 1938. The notorious, catastrophic storm wiped out Chalybes' remaining wooden structures, leaving the stone hulks of the blast furnace and roasting ovens.

The site got a final reprieve, however, when it was acquired by the Roxbury Land Trust and turned into a preserve. It was then declared a National Historic Landmark in 1979.

Today, Mine Hill Preserve comprises 360 acres traversed by paths dotted with Chalybes' ruins. A main loop follows a "donkey trail"—the animals dragged stone along it during the town's brief heyday—as well as old farm and quarry roads. Visitors first come to the giant blast furnace dominating its patch of forest. Even in its diminished state, it is somehow majestic, crafted of enormous slabs of brick blackened and pockmarked with drill holes and chisel marks. Its three entryways are curved to points, giving the structure an almost church-like architectural quality. It is flanked by roasting ovens sitting further up the hill.

Continuing on, visitors pass towering quarry piles, cross a stone quarry bridge, then come to the heart of the former mining area. There remain numerous shafts now caged over or enclosed by giant crib-like grate. These are to prevent the curious from wandering inside, while also providing unperturbed shelter for little brown bats, northern long-eared bats, big brown bats, and pipistrelles drawn by the median 50-to-55-degree temperature of the shafts.

Even though they have been sealed, visitors can walk up to their enclosures and feel the cool air emanating from within. A half-mile of subterranean tunnels still exists beneath; as do iron rails once used to transport quarried ore. Even as they serve as physical manifestations of the once, if fleetingly, vibrant mining town, the chasms hold their memories within their dark depths.

DANIELS VILLAGE/KILLINGLY

Located along Five Mile River in the town of Killingly that tightly hugs the Rhode Island border, the former town of Daniels holds an important distinction in Connecticut history, and today serves as an important archaeological site.

The town dates to roughly 1725, when Isaac Parks erected a home and gristmill on Five Mile's north bank. Much of the land in the area had been previously held in common; it was divided in the early 1720s, opening it up to settlement. In turn, an increase in settlers required more mills to support them. Jared Talbot and David Perry built a sawmill, tanyard, and dwelling house just upstream from Park's Mill in 1760; this would become known as Talbot's Mills. Several other mills were also erected by the end of the eighteenth century.

But 1813 brought the most significant growth to Daniels Village: That year, local landowners combined forces with a group of investors from Rhode Island to establish a cotton mill. It came to be known as Howe's Factory, and it was one of the earliest textile mills in Connecticut. A store, blacksmith shop, and three separate mills sprung up around it, as did at least nine tenement houses. A footbridge was also built across the Five Mile River.

The mill was acquired by the Daniels family in 1845, thus giving the town its name. It prospered for another sixteen years until the mill buildings burned to their foundations in 1861. They were not rebuilt, and locals started moving elsewhere. The Daniels' finally sold the property in 1888, and by the early twentieth century most of its buildings had collapsed or been ravaged by vandals.

The former town may have continued deteriorating into the earth—but in 1978, it was granted reprieve when it was placed on the National Register of Historic Places. It has since been the site of excavations and historical studies and is identified as an important historical link to the growth and subsequent decline of New England history. Notably, Albert F. Bartovics of Brown University has traced its development, and Robert Gradie, a UConn archaeologist, have unearthed numerous artifacts, including textile implements that predate the Civil War.

Today, the privately-owned site still retains the nineteenth century dam, foundational remnants of the cotton mill and worker housing, and portions of the channels beneath the grist and cotton mills. They are but remnants of the historically important site—but, importantly, they will be preserved for posterity.

TWENTY-TWO

PLEASURE BEACH

Not a Pleasure Anymore

IT WAS LIKE WALKING THROUGH A BURNED AND BOMBED, APOCA-
lyptic wasteland.

Humble cottages prone to constant wind and wuthering storms
were battered and deteriorating, some tilting into the mawing
earth, broken windows bandaged up with plywood. Debris of all
imagination was scattered everywhere—inside, outside, along the
shoreline, in the beach grass.

What sidewalks were left were cracked and heaved into volcanic-
like structures by the shifting, tempestuous earth. Ivy and other
rampant greenery were slowly strangling everything they had so long
been denied. A one-time ballroom, pavilion, and structures that had
once housed joyful, rollicking carousels and bumper cars were literal
shells, crumbling and stripped of their contents.

All this degradation can be attributed to the flick of a cigarette.

On June 16, 1996, a motorist crossing the wooden bridge
between Pleasure Beach and mainland Bridgeport tossed a smol-
dering cigarette butt out their window, thus igniting—or so it's
been asserted—a blaze that destroyed the overpass and stranded

locals and visitors. The narrow point, whose status had been ever shifting to begin with, effectively became an island.

Hours later, the flames were finally doused—but a 100-year-old tradition was ultimately lost. Cut off from the mainland with no chance of a new bridge ever being built, residents would filter away, then be forced to leave. Visitors would have no way to get across, lest they walk three-some-odd miles, use their own boats or charter one—and anyway, concession stands, a ballroom, and amusement rides would be shut down, their contents eventually dismantled and ferried away. There would be no real reason to visit; in fact, the consensus would eventually be to stay away.

TENUOUS LINKS

Until that fateful 1996 conflagration, Pleasure Beach had been a charming beachside community and tourist attraction. The Bridge-port portion of a barrier beach, it extends 2.5 miles west of the (fittingly titled) cape Point No Point on the skinny arm of land. When the tide is high, the beach to its west returns to the ocean, thus facilitating the need for a bridge connecting to the mainland.

When the growing city of Bridgeport absorbed the borough of West Stratford in 1889, the deal included this thirty-seven-acre triangle at the mouth of the harbor.

As legend had it, Captain Kidd had buried treasure on the bar-rier island—an oft asserted claim throughout the eastern seaboard. Local liquor dealers J. H. McMahon and P. W. Wren capitalized on this bit of folklore, turning the island into an amusement park in three years' time.

From then (1892) until 1958, the beach was home to the attraction that bore its name (or vice versa). It did have two brief periods under a different nomenclature: In 1904, George C. Tilyou, the proprietor of Steeplechase Park on Coney Island, took over as owner. It was then dubbed "Steeplechase Island" after the unique ride housed on its park that involved carousel-style horses racing down a metal track. It would retain that name until 1919, then operate for a short while as "Sea Breeze Island."

The year 1908 brought with it one of the first ravaging fires. Baseball players had gathered for a game on the park's playing fields when someone (player, spectator, no one can be sure) carelessly disposed of a cigarette in the dry beach grass. This burned much of the park, including the popular steeplechase ride. It's been said that the players continued on for five innings as the park burned, even hitting foul balls into the bleachers as they smoldered.

The city of Bridgeport came into possession of the park in 1919, expanding and improving it with boardwalks, and installing a miniature railroad, roller skating rink, roller coaster, carousel, bicycle racing track, and other simple rides. The Pleasure Beach Park would eventually encompass a whole host of amusements: a popular rollercoaster called the Sky Rocket, a Ferris wheel, toboggan ride, funhouse, kiddie park, softball and baseball fields, bowling alley, mini golf course, vaudeville theater, the Polka Dot Playhouse, convention hall with a 2,000 seat capacity, restaurants, an open-air arena, and landscaped gardens. The local WICC 600 radio station also located a transmitter on the island.

One of the beach's greatest attractions, though, was its grand ballroom. The largest in New England at the time, it was host to such jazz age stars as Glenn Miller, Benny Goodman, Artie Shaw, Tommy Dorsey, and Gene Krupa. An adjacent dancing pavilion was outfitted with a maple floor and glass-sided bell towers. It was, as one resident described it to local historians, a "jumpin'" place. As a prime example of this, on Memorial Day weekend 1938, it was estimated that roughly 30,000 residents from surrounding Fairfield County flocked to its shores.

The park, and the ensuing summer cottages that were built up around it, survived and thrived without a permanent bridge for fifty-five years. Summer residents and visitors utilized ferry services, a drawbridge, and a swing bridge to get back and forth. It wasn't until 1947 that the U.S. Army Corps of Engineers built a bridge connecting Pleasure Beach to the opposite shore. This allowed passage for cars and pedestrians.

"Pleasure Beach was a terrific place for ordinary working-class people to spend the day in a resort-like atmosphere," Mary Witkowski, author of *Bridgeport on the Sound* and one-time head of historical collections at the Bridgeport Public Library, told the website oldpleasurebeachct.com. "With a long stretch of beach, wonderful amusement rides and tons of good food, (it) was a nice haven away from the sooty, hot city."

Still, beginning in the 1950s, it apparently began to lose its draw; fewer people meant less upkeep, and the park began falling into disrepair. This was exacerbated by an ensuing string of fires, which were more destructive than they might have been if on the mainland. Due to its remote location and limited access, emergency personnel had a hard time getting to the site of blazes in time, so hungry flames often entirely consumed buildings until completely satiated. This was the fate of many of the park's concessions, roller coaster, midway, and, in spectacular fashion, its grand ballroom. As fire blazed and crackled in the night sky like fireworks, hundreds of Bridgeport natives gathered on the shore to watch.

Fire ravaged the park in 1953, 1957, 1965, 1972, 1973, and 1996. On more than one occasion, these were the result of discarded cigarettes, but faulty wiring, portable stoves, and firebug vandals were also identified as culprits. As Bridgeport had a busy waterfront, other calamities involved boats smashing into the bridge—their overconfident captains misjudging the clearance—or catching fire while carrying hazardous cargo.

Then there was the inferno on Father's Day 1996 that marooned Pleasure Beach for good. At that time, the barrier beach had grown to forty-four cottages.

On that pleasant Sunday afternoon, a few hundred residents and visitors were sunbathing, picnicking, and fishing from the beach's pier. Others were planning to attend a matinee performance of Neil Simon's *Laughter on the 23rd Floor* at the Polka Dot Playhouse. Suddenly, flashes and sparks flicked the sky above the bridge. These were stoked by thick coats of creosote that was meant to protect wooden pilings and substructure from the salty gnawings of the ocean. People watched helplessly from both shores. On the mainland side, firefighters attempted to quench it. But the water from their hoses couldn't reach the bridge's beams and supports, and the wind was toying with them, tugging the flames back and forth. Beach residents took action with an impromptu bucket brigade, which helped contain the fire.

Efforts on both sides eventually snuffed the inferno—but only after it had blazed for more than two hours, charring two hundred feet of the bridge beyond recognition.

Along with the stranded residents and visitors, more than 180 vehicles were trapped, and another 200 boats could not pass through the harbor into Long Island Sound because the bridge's swing span had been damaged. Eventually, their way was cleared, and cars were ferried off the island. People were stranded for the night until a transport was arranged to return them to the other side. Hoping to enliven a dour situation, the actors who had come over to stage the Simon play stayed true to the precept that "the show must go on." They did just that for a captive, if distressed and distracted, audience.

After that, Pleasure Beach's fate was a tenuous one, as officials vacillated between saving it, redeveloping it, or allowing it to go to ruin. As this indecisiveness ensued over more than a decade, it was the latter that has ultimately played out.

WASHED OUT

Not long after the annihilating conflagration, locals decried that, just months earlier, there had been an allocation of funds from the state to replace the bridge—but no projects had ever moved forward. If they had, their homes might have been saved.

The city estimated the cost to repair the bridge at $20 to $30 million; three years later, that estimate was significantly reduced to $8 million. But it was not economically feasible, according to the city council. Instead, the body announced that residents' leases would not be renewed and that the island would have to be vacated. What's more, when locals tried to negotiate a purchase of the land, they were refused. The city council justified that decision: In light of the devastating bridge fire and without a connecting bridge, it would be difficult to protect them from similar disaster or crime. Police cruisers and fire trucks would be significantly delayed in the event of any emergency.

Going forward, this meant that Pleasure Beach could only be accessed by private boat, or after a three-to-four-mile trek by foot. Bridgeport officials considered a ferry service to relink the beach with the city, but this idea was ultimately rejected due to concerns with parking, as well as the need to have a Coast Guard registered captain manning the shuttle.

Over the years, proposals for the beach's renewal included a hotel/conference center, a maritime amusement park, an aquarium, night club and shops—even a nudist camp. Disney expressed interest in the park for a regional entertainment center; Donald Trump for a "world-class" theme park and casino; Steve Wynn for luxury condos. But nothing materialized, and people began to give up. Residents packed up and ferried what belongings they could across the harbor to Bridgeport. The park's once rollicking buildings were stripped of their more valuable contents and boarded up. The carousel was disassembled, its horses rescued by conservationists and relocated to Beardsley Zoo in Bridgeport.

From there, things just got progressively worse.

In 2007, Bridgeport officials finally ordered all the cottages vacated. There had been a few holdouts; they were now legally required to leave. In coming years, several of the cottages burned, the casualty of arson or accidental fires set by a growing number of squatters. Firefighters resorting to using hand-carried gear to fight the flames—they could not navigate a fire truck to the scene, proving city officials' assertion to that very fact. It was also discovered that many cottages still had attached propane tanks, which was extremely perilous for emergency workers. Many of these were later removed.

Curiously, in 2009, an unauthorized demotion by Burns Construction Company took place; the carousel, bumper car area, and bandstand were leveled without permission or permit. Not much else has been reported on the incident.

The following year brought a bright spot in an otherwise dark future: $1.9 million in federal funding was allotted to clean Pleasure Beach, upgrade its docks and infrastructure, and cover the cost of a pair of water taxis. In March 2010, a temporary road was built along a stretch of shoreline to the cottages, and another $909,000 in federal stimulus money was used to clear them. By 2011, nearly all of the structures were gone.

Every couple of years since then has brought talk of revitalization, with officials tentatively circling the can without kicking it down the road. In 2014, the beach re-opened to the public, with the taxis ferrying visitors over from a fishing pier on Seaview Avenue. A new paved walkway had been installed, the boardwalk had been repaired, and the site included a refurbished pavilion and "relaxation area" with several bathrooms, showers, picnic tables, and a limited concession stand. But it was a temporary revival: The city shut down ferry services and even purportedly put the site up for sale.

What it has lacked in the human element, though, has enabled others to thrive: Notably, Pleasure Beach is a protected refuge for endangered birds such as the piping plover and osprey, as well as the prickly pear cactus and southern sea lavender. As such, sections of the beach are roped off seasonally to protect these species and their nesting areas, as well as delicate beach dunes. Those found trespassing on them face significant fines.

Decades after the fateful fire, the narrow spit is estimated to contain more than 25 percent of Connecticut's remaining undeveloped beachfront—which, no matter where you go, is always at a premium.

TIDES OF RUIN

Before demolition crews moved in to effectively destruct the destruction, though, visiting the former park and its environs was a surreal experience—a backdrop right out of an end-of-times disaster movie, and a portend, perhaps, of what humankind has in store.

Even before the connector bridge burned, Pleasure Beach had begun to attract a seedier element. Increasingly abandoned, it became a haven for squatters and drug users, and nearly every building had been vandalized in one form or another. There were even reports of the discovery of body parts stuffed into large plastic bags.

The structures that remained were disintegrated, concave, collapsed, seemingly bombed out—which in a sense, they were, only not all at once in a blaze of ammunition, but achingly over time by the elements. The carousel and Dodge-'Em car enclosures were bereft of their horses and padded jalopies. Greenery claimed their buttresses and their rounded and octagonal roofs were collapsing inward, the crumbling remnants of their chassis whispering of the lively places they once were. In the former playhouse, rotting rows of seats maintained their gaze toward an equally decomposing stage. The pavilion was an emptied, hulking frame where only shadows walked. Everything was scrawled with graffiti.

The ground, at least that which wasn't wildly overgrown, was a carpet of cigarette butts and trash of every kind imaginable. Asphalt was fissured and cratered. Rotting plywood and rusting nails sat in gargantuan piles.

The remaining cottages were in similarly decaying states: Windows that hadn't been boarded up like open wounds were smashed; front doors were bashed in or rusted off their hinges, creaky and askance. Unpassable porches threatened to devour prone ankles and legs. Parked outside their garages were lawn tractors that would never again mow patches of lawn—in fact, the grass was finally exacting its revenge.

Inside, contents were strewn about, hit by tornadoes of vandals. Soiled, time-toppled chairs and sofas; all manner of children's toys and water-bloated books; felled microwaves, stoves, and refrigerators—the latter even containing left-behind condiments. Pantries remained stocked with time-stained jars and cans, kitchens with essential implements such as rolling pins, dish drainers, cleaning supplies, even moldering paper towels. Also abandoned were rusted stationary bicycles, a rotary dial phone still mounted to the wall, a stand-up piano, ivory keys uneven and browned like rotted teeth, even sepia family pictures.

Walking through the abandoned, ravaged place fueled adrenaline, unease, anxiety—active imaginations could conjure up the many horror movie-like scenarios occurring against this backdrop. It was no longer the pleasurable place that it had been, but perhaps the tide will turn in its favor once again.

TWENTY-THREE

HOLY LAND

Seeking Salvation

TREK UP AN ASPHALT HILL, DUCK THROUGH ONE OF THREE SQUAT arches, and you find yourself in a miniaturized mystery.

The slope above you is cluttered with dozens of tiny white buildings, cutouts, and dioramas. Time, vandalism, and weather have tilted many of them haphazardly; others have been toppled, crumbled, or reduced to mere rubble.

Simple white monuments resembling tombstones stud the grassy earth; as you ascend concrete steps cut into the hillside, they inform you along the way: "Jesus Meets His Mother," "Jesus Is Helped by Simon," "Jesus Falls a Second Time."

Elsewhere are felled signs scrawled or etched with tenets such as "Husbands Love Your Wives" or "The Rainbow Praises Those Who Made It." A life-sized statue of Jesus stands incongruously against the Lilliputian backdrop, beckoning with outstretched arms. Other mini effigies stand bereft of heads or have been softened to the point of crumbling by the elements. Simple, mid-sized wooden crosses are tacked everywhere, tilted to and fro.

A much larger, yet still piously simple, crucifix stands at the apex of all this. As you gaze up at it and then back down the hill at the central-Connecticut city of Waterbury, you can't help but wonder: What is this place? And why is it here?

Holy Land is wholly unique—as a theme park, a landmark, an abandoned place, a revitalization project.

Located on eighteen acres atop Pine Hill, the one-time religiously themed destination attracted tens of thousands of visitors a year with its pious miniaturization of biblical stories. Then, for decades, it sat neglected, becoming as overgrown by Mother Nature as it was by vandalism and other crime. Now, it is undergoing its own resurrection.

Throughout its manifestations, its illuminated crucifix has remained a constant. This is as much a symbol of its religious and physical perseverance as it has been a stoking of curiosity—some have likened the cross to a physical question mark. And indeed, Holy Land has attracted the religious, the curiosity-seeking, and the lovers of the abandoned and the kitsch alike—ultimately achieving its envisioner's goal to provoke contemplation.

GENESIS

That conceiver was John Baptist Greco: Holy Land USA was his own passion play.

Born to Italian immigrants and raised Roman Catholic, the Waterbury native initially planned to go into the priesthood. But he diverted to law, earning his degree from Yale University. He was admitted to the Connecticut bar in 1926. As he practiced law in his home city, he became known for his soft-spoken piousness; he often provided free services to immigrant neighbors and friends or translated legal documents for them. (However, as dictated by his religion, he would not take divorce cases.)

In 1930, Greco discovered a channel for his spirituality in Catholic Campaigners for Christ. He founded the Connecticut chapter of the Christian apologetics group, which proselytized its values through open-air lectures such as "Prayer, Its Meaning and Value" and "Why Catholics Honor the Blessed Virgin." At the same time, he began envisioning Holy Land USA, which he intended to serve as Connecticut's own (miniaturized) version of Jerusalem or Bethlehem.

Some might have considered the idea tacky or falsely pious, but it was entirely sensible to Greco. God-fearing Italians worship numerous saints and have a tradition of giving public expression to their spirituality—this via statuary in their homes, in passion plays, or at festivals. In that sense, Greco envisioned Holy Land as a means to reach the general public and "popularize" Christ's story by providing them with tangible symbols to contemplate. Physical manifestations of biblical events—no matter how small—could help make them seem more real and attainable.

As stated in a sign eventually erected by the Campaigners at the Holy Land gate: They were "A group of men who present a pictorial story of the life of Christ from the cradle to the Cross—it is our prayerful wish that the project will provide a pleasant way to increase your knowledge of God's Own Book and bring you closer to Him."

The installation of a thirty-two foot "Peace Cross" in November 1956 marked the first phase of the project. It was lit alternating green and red; green as a symbol of hope; red as a reminder of Soviet communism and aggression. In contrast to that bold, over-sized symbol, the park itself would be scaled down and detailed.

While running his full-time private law practice during the day, Greco spent evenings and weekends on Pine Hill along with a loyal band of volunteers. He funded the project with his own savings and inheritances, and began to study the Bible, maps, and photographs to ensure that Holy Land would be as true to biblical teachings as possible. He even eventually made research trips to Jerusalem and Bethlehem to collect additional impressions, as well as soil and rocks to incorporate into exhibits.

"Bethlehem Village," as it was originally known, was officially dedicated and opened on December 11, 1958. At its peak, it contained roughly two hundred buildings and attracted more than 40,000 visitors a year. Greco himself, a lifelong bachelor who lived on the property, preached God's love through a megaphone and even led visitors on tours.

By its very unique nature, the site could sell itself. But the ever-passionate Greco and his fellow Campaigners generated additional buzz through various publicity efforts. Capitalizing on the site's location high above Interstate 84, Greco also mimicked the iconic "Hollywood" sign: Huge white letters were staked into the ground to dramatically spell out "Holy Land U.S.A."

Bob Chinn, a grounds manager for the attraction, stated the obvious in a 2001 interview with *The New York Times* when he called Greco a "very spiritual man." But he also lauded him for his vision, saying that "he felt (that) no one, no matter the race, creed, or color, should be separated. He wanted a place for all people to sit and be peaceful."

PILGRIMAGE

To that end, Holy Land visitors could walk the biblical stories as they unfurled along Pine Hill and beneath it.

A 200-foot-long cinderblock tunnel drove home the grimness and despair of the catacombs. Narrow paths led to various dollhouse-sized structures, from the rugged mound of the "grotto of the holy family" to the barred-up dugout of the nativity scene revealing a wooden cutout of Mary, Moses, baby Jesus, and the Star of Bethlehem. A procession of monuments chronicled the aching process of the Stations of the Cross; replicas of the three crosses on Calvary flanked one another at the crest of the park's slope.

There was also once a creche, eight feet high by eighteen feet deep, outfitted with statues of the blessed infant and assembled animals and Magi. An oversized Bible painted red, white, and blue was permanently open to the Ten Commandments. Concrete tablets and monuments scattered around the site proclaimed: "We Are the Body of Christ. If One Member Suffers, All Members Suffer." There was also a cast-metal Christ on a cross; yellow-painted golden calves.

These tiny holy displays were constructed of all manner of objects easily obtained, salvaged, scavenged, cast-out, and refurbished. Greco and his acolytes were industrious and creative, using cobbled-together odds and ends including appliances, soup pots and utensils, hand railings, even televisions and radios. These were combined with stones, cinderblocks, bricks, clay, plywood, plaster, stainless steel, tons of cement, and salvaged architectural flourishes.

Store mannequins stood in for Christian martyrs. Local churches or Catholic organizations donated exhibition materials, and pillars from the 1964–1965 World's Fair's Vatican pavilion even made their way to Holy Land after the closing of the exhibition. But not all came cheap: One statue of the Good Shepherd was imported from Italy at a cost of $1,000.

Today, the tumbledown miniaturized assemblage hearkens a sort of religious mini golf course. Diminutive replicas of chapels, catacombs, and Israelite villages stand in rickety procession along the slopes; some have been painted afresh, while others have been subverted by vines, or toppled into scattered heaps of metal, concrete, and wood. The structures in their various states of decay are interspersed with crosses rustic and white in all their simplicity. "Amen" and "God is Love" are affirmed throughout, painted on walls and rocks or etched into them.

There's a tiny squat depiction of the inn that turned away Joseph and Mary, its "no vacancy" sign chipped off to near eligibility. Herod's Palace is but a tiny white shack two feet tall; it is constructed of scrap wood, its veranda with its thin wooden spindles askew. A cylindrical outcropping of brick and mortar stands in as the tower of Babel. Arched acropolises lean and lurch. A disintegrated diorama that once depicted the full glory of the last supper is left with just painted-on remnants of Jesus' words: "This is my commandment, that you love one another," and "Take and eat, this is my body."

The giant letters of the "Holy Land U.S.A." sign is weathered and weary. Decorative bricks are assembled to urgingly plea that people "HONOR GOD."

A true-to-size effigy of Jesus with pleading hands is perhaps one of the most poignant and reflective of the curious, enigmatic site. An entreaty etched into its base is half-buried in the earth and grass: "Come to me all you who labor and are hardened and I will. . . ."

The site is all at once surreal, sacred, visually captivating, and disheartening. It is a hallowed ground of multifaceted intentions.

EXODUS AND RESURRECTION

Perhaps as a portend of things to come, in 1972, the Archdiocese of Hartford assigned two nuns from the Religious Teachers Filippini to assist Greco in operating Holy Land. They gave tours and helped with upkeep, even assisting Greco as his health continued to fail until his death in 1986. By then the site had already been closed for two years; Greco's plans to refurbish and reopen it went unfulfilled.

Without his guidance, and as a sort of physical manifestation of his loss, Holy Land soon began to fall into ruin. And as abandoned places often do—especially one as unique as a crumbling former religious theme park—the property began to attract curiosity seekers, vandals, and seedier populations. Human and weather-inflicted damage continued to take its dramatic toll. The former park became notorious, even more so due to grisly incidents including a rape and murder in 2010 at the very base of its landmark cross.

Over the years, there was ongoing debate about its future: Some suggested the park be preserved for its folk-art significance; others, including a Hartford archbishop and the local Knights of Columbus, proposed revitalizations. All the while, the sisters from Religious Teachers Filippini continued to hold regular prayer meetings and other events, even as they seemed reticent to take any action on future plans.

Finally, in 2013, Waterbury mayor Neil O'Leary and car dealer Fred Blasius purchased Holy Land from Filippini for $350,000. They announced their intent to restore the site, and started by installing a new, fifty-seven-foot-tall, internally lit LED cross. They also cleared rampant trees and underbrush and made cosmetic improvements in the way of new coats of paint for some of the Lilliputian buildings.

On September 14, 2014, thirty years after its closure, Holy Land reopened to the public. This was heralded by an inaugural mass. It is now open to visitors during daylight hours, and its owning nonprofit "Holy Land USA—Waterbury" says it plans to hold regular Christian prayer services, concerts, and other mountaintop events.

So, it seems, Holy Land may finally have a much-deserved resurrection all its own.

PART VI

RHODE ISLAND

Born down in a dad man's town . . .
—BRUCE SPRINGSTEEN

At just 1,214 square miles and spanning roughly forty-eight miles north to south and thirty-seven miles east to west, it has the distinction of being the smallest state in the union.

But while it might be diminutive in size, it is big in history and culture.

It was the first colony in America to declare independence, on May 4, 1776—a full two months before the U.S. Declaration of Independence. Yet because of its hesitation to adopt the U.S. Constitution, it was the last of the thirteen original colonies to ratify it (and thus be granted statehood) on May 29, 1790. It is considered to be the birthplace of the American Industrial Revolution: Samuel Slater built the first textile mill in Pawtucket in 1793. Newport on a finger of land on its coast hosted America's Cup for many years and is home to renowned Gilded Age mansions including the Breakers, which was built in 1895 to resemble a Renaissance palace.

Also, despite its small land mass, it has its share of ghost towns, too.

TWENTY-FOUR

HANTON

The "Lost City"

LEAVES CRINKLING BENEATH YOUR FEET, FORGE YOUR OWN PATH through the quintessentially New England woods.

If you're diligent—or perhaps stubborn—enough, your wanderings may eventually bring you to a half-dozen or so foundations, portions of rock walls, and what look to be wells being reclaimed by the earth. You might also come across a giant stone slab covered with moss—likely what was previously part of a dam—and even a burial site whose broken markers have been whitewashed by the elements to near illegibility.

Welcome to what was once Hanton City.

Some Smithfield residents, lovers of the abandoned, and ghost hunters know it as "The Lost City"; many aren't aware of its fading existence (or history) at all. Today, its former location is notoriously difficult to find. The dwindling remains of its physical presence are sprawled across an area of woods off Hanton City trail in northern Smithfield, but it takes much scouting to (perhaps literally) stumble across it. For those familiar with the area, the abandoned, overgrown town may have once crossed the Douglas Pike area and ran up into North Smithfield.

The name is actually a misnomer; the town in the northern-central section of the Ocean State close to the Massachusetts border could hardly be considered a "city" even when it was inhabited.

And even that fact is up for conjecture.

Also known over time as "Island Woods," "Cedar Swamp," "Rumbly" and even "Ghost City," and "Haunted City" because of its purported paranormal activity, the history of Hanton City is abounding with unknowns and curiosities. Possibly of all of New England's many ghost towns, it has the most perplexing, intertwining, and contradicting back stories; it is a lost hamlet of much folklore.

For years, legends have swirled around the reasons for its settlement: It was a haven for British loyalists around the time of the American Revolution; a refuge for escaped slaves; a banishment spot for the poor and destitute, mentally ill, lepers or those stricken with other communicable diseases. Simpler explanations are that it was made up of like-minded settlers seeking solace from the more bustling adjacent Smithfield or other, larger, nearby locales.

It is also unclear exactly when it was settled—or by whom. Some locals have pointed to early Providence records and deeds books that indicate that a Benjamin Hearnton Sr., who arrived in the Rhode Island capital between 1647 and 1651, acquired common land ten miles north of Providence through a series of transactions. It was a land described as "part upland, part swamp" that Benjamin deeded in parcels to his four sons. Hanton is then said to be a derivation of Hearnton—which, some say, by the twentieth century had morphed into the spelling "Harrington." Others, meanwhile, including Smithfield-area historian Jim Ignasher, have concluded that the town was first settled by three English loyalist families—the Hantons, Paines, and Shippees. As was a regular practice at the time, they were deeded the land as a payment for their service in King Philip's War, which lasted from 1675 to 1678.

"They were English as were many settlers to Smithfield," Ignasher writes, "of a social class known as yeoman or freemen, which put them near the bottom of the social ladder of the day."

Since land ownership was a symbol of status and provided voting rights, many such "lower class" individuals were incentivized to accept, and settle, free parcels in the untamed wild.

POOR BUT INDUSTRIOUS

In any case, the consensus seems to be that the town was settled around the time of King Philip's War, then abandoned by the mid-to-late 1800s. Before that (as would be expected), it was occupied by natives.

Over time it was called "Island Woods" and "Cedar Swamp" because its high, rock-studded, thickly wooded hills rose up out of bogs and wetlands. The "Rumbly" title came about because of its many (at the time) steep, rough roads traversing rocky soil. Its out-of-the-way location and rough landscape have since given rise to many questions about why it was settled in the first place—and the many aforementioned rumors.

Its settlers were said to be poor but industrious, using as many of the giant rocks spotting the landscape, just as they were, for their homes and gathering spaces. They quarried stone that was then sent to the roughly 15-mile-away Providence and farmed what fertile land they could.

After a season's harvest, they were said to have used what's known as a "threshing rock"—in their case an enormous boulder with a naturally formed hollow. In this they would use a flail to separate grain from husk. Natives were believed to have utilized the same giant rock to crush their corn.

Many of the town's men also worked as tanners and, later, boot-makers who sold their handmade goods in more nearby populated cities. As a further source of income, they maintained a small shed on the edge of town that was always stocked with bread and a bit of rum. This was meant as a spot of rest for weary travelers passing through from Woonsocket or beyond—the hope being that they would show their appreciation with a coin or two.

But as the decades passed, for whatever reason, Hanton became a sparser and sparser community, its population dwindling until fading out completely.

According to Ignasher, the earliest documented investigation into its history, and what happened to its residents, was reported by the *Providence Journal* in 1889. An uncredited reporter traveled from Providence to Smithfield, a trip that required a train ride followed by what was undoubtedly a bumpy journey by horse-drawn carriage. A local guide then led them to a "small shanty" on the outskirts of town occupied by 80-year-old Thomas Hanton and his sister.

In an article later headlined "The Buried City," the reporter described the two as the "last of the Hantons."

The octogenarian told the reporter that his town "was a lively and enterprising place, when he was young," and that it had been in its prime in the 1730s. He also corroborated stories of its residents' economic situation, saying they were so destitute that when couples were wed, their justice of the peace would be paid not with money, but a "good meal" and a jug of rum.

But time has a way of eroding memory, and those with first-hand knowledge of the hamlet began to disappear. As Ignasher notes, despite the *Journal* article and the historical information it contained, "by the early twentieth century, what happened to the people of Hanton City was once again a mystery."

For whatever reason, interest was once again ignited in the 1930s, when local researchers and reporters interviewed ninety-year-old Edwin C. Harris of Smithfield. Then in the 1970s, Martha O. Tanner of *The Observer* explored the abandoned site. The local paper published several pictures of Hanton's ruins, which were then much more pronounced and discoverable. These included the gigantic threshing rock; four stone pillars near a cellar hole eventually identified as what was once a corncrib (to store and dry corn); and the crumbling remains of a farm site with a large stone wall fording a stream.

A caption for the above read: "The rocks in the wall are big and no doubt took a great deal of labor to move into place."

Still, now, as then, many continue to ask: Why did it slowly disappear?

Some explanations that have been bandied about are that the settlement was wiped out by waves of disease or that it became wayside as new traveling routes cut through it.

More likely, though, the rough conditions simply became too much for its residents as Rhode Island's growing civilization provided more alternatives for economic survival. The Industrial Revolution was also likely a significant death knell; as was the case with many artisans in small towns, the introduction of mills that could produce previously handmade products much more cheaply and faster made them obsolete.

As Tom Hanton told the *Journal* in 1899: "They had all got poor, and sold out to anybody, and died off."

Whatever the answer, as Hanton continues to disintegrate into the earth and fade from memory, it holds fast to its secrets.

Twenty-Five

FOUNTAIN SPRING/SKEETERVILLE

Leading Industry

But Hanton wasn't the only close-to-Smithfield, now-expired hamlet.

Another town that was founded in relative tandem but existed for far longer—and was much more prosperous—was known by several idiosyncratic titles, most notably Reaper's Brook, Ripper's Brook, Skeeterville, and Fountain Spring.

While Pawtucket to the northeast may hold the distinction as the birthplace of the American Industrial Revolution—Samuel Slater built the first textile mill there in 1793—Skeeterville was the site of the state's second fulling mill. It is also believed to be the first mill in the country to manufacture parts for burgeoning textile mills.

The town's origins date to 1663, when the Rhode Island colony was only twenty-seven years old and the area now comprising present-day Smithfield was still considered a wild outland to Providence. That year, William Hawkins was granted fifty acres in the area that would eventually become Skeeterville. Hawkins' family had the distinction of being among Rhode Island's first settlers, arriving in Providence in 1663 with state founder Roger Williams.

This granting came with the stipulation that Hawkins improve the land, live there for at least three years, and receive the consent of Providence town officials before selling it.

As Ignasher notes in a history of the area, it was understood that, for the young state to thrive, people had to be willing to leave civilization to populate wild areas, and free land created incentive because of its association with wealth and opportunity.

It was said at the time that, "he shall this summer go there, cut hay and build houses there and so also go there in the winter ensuing to inhabit, possessing the land."

This he did, building a dwelling and barn beside the Nipmuc Trail—which connected Providence and Connecticut—along Ripper's Brook (now Reaper's Brook). Others soon followed.

Around the turn of the century, Hawkins partnered with Daniel Williams to build a fulling mill, which was where debris was removed from raw wool before spinning. At the time, the typical, time-consuming practice was to home-spin wool on a wheel, then weave it into cloth on a loom and sew it into clothing. Previously, the state's only other fulling mill was in Apponaug village in Warwick, built by John Micarter in 1695.

Englishman Robert Saunders helped build and operate the mill for more than two decades before building his own nearby, creating the dam Factory Pond to power it.

Hawkins' mill, meanwhile, went through several iterations with the centuries, being first converted to a sawmill, then a machine shop manufacturing cotton machinery, then a cotton weaving plant. The town's largest building soon went up: a three-story stone mill powered by Hawkins Pond.

By 1850, according to the U.S. Census, this mill had thirty-two looms and 1,080 spindles operated by eleven males and fifteen females. Then known as Skeeterville, the town also had a store and several houses.

"INDEED LOST"

But over the decades the cotton industry dwindled, and in the 1890s the three-story mill, stone buildings and outbuildings and several millhouses were sold to a Greenville businessman. By then the site had ceased operations, and efforts to revive it were futile. The property changed hands several more times and was used sporadically for storing ice, then apples.

Its final owner, Fred W. Thrift, had intentions to convert the property into a summer colony, and had its largest house relocated to the top of a hill, where he lived for sixteen years. A visiting reporter described the view from "the big house" as "picturesque in the distance," but its foreground full of cottages "as homely and as squalid as mill cottages usually appear, in city or country, although not without advantages of their own."

Thrift removed the old fulling mill, and in the 1920s, several more buildings were razed.

A 1927 news report described Skeeterville as a "'Lost Village that was indeed lost.'"

"Only the half-ruined remains of the old mill testify to the former busy character of the place," the report continued, noting that its two other mills had "disappeared," and there was "no trace" of stores that operated there, while only two small cottages in addition to the large house on the hill remained.

"The casual visitor of today would never dream that here, for nearly a century, was once the busiest little village," the writeup concluded.

Today, all evidence of the once thrumming mill town is gone; it has been replaced by homes with intertwining streets such as Reaper Court and Fountain Spring Lane.

And what of that "busiest little village's" ever-changing, colorful names? The origins for Ripper's Brook and Reaper's Brook, with their hints at morbidity, are unknown. The Skeeterville moniker is a little more humorous: an homage, of sorts, to the town's significant mosquito population (no doubt as the result of its two ponds). And Fountain Spring came about in the 1870s because, it was said, many of its homes had springs in their cellars.

There is one decided mystery that endures with the vanished town: its missing cemetery. A *Journal* article in 1918 described the cemetery as on a "prominence" overlooking a pond, with about twenty-five head and foot stones with "nearly obliterated markings." "Only one stone was readable due to it having fallen over face down," the article read. The name it bore was "Sanders."

As Ignasher notes, a survey in 1919 of every grave in every cemetery in Smithfield overlooked the Skeeterville cemetery— most likely due to its advanced state of deterioration—and those who try to look for it today have had no success in finding it.

Thus, the once prosperous Skeeterville does not even bear an epitaph.

TWENTY-SIX

SCITUATE

Doused Out

PICTURE YOURSELF IN YOUR HOME, YOUR SANCTUARY—MAYBE ONE with the warm comfort and feel of many generations; maybe one that is newer to you and your family. On the outside, it might look like just a wooden structure with four walls and a roof, but it is where you've shared memories, moments, and rites of passage both good and bad.

Now imagine being told that you must vacate that home in the name of progress. That it would soon be effectively drowned so that more so-called civilized people in a city nearly a dozen miles away would have a clean, constant source of drinking water.

This is the story of Scituate—as it was for the residents of Flagstaff, Maine, and the towns now lost to time at the bottom of the Quabbin and Wachusett reservoirs in Massachusetts, not to mention countless other communities across the country.

In the 1920s, several once-thriving villages representing nearly half of the town of Scituate were engulfed in thirty-nine billion gallons of water. This was to provide a reliable source of tap water to the capital of Providence (and eventually, a significant portion of the state of Rhode Island).

Since its creation, the reservoir has been a central feature of the 54.8-square-mile town, forming what could be described as an enormous "Y" from above. And within its depths are the disintegrated ruins of houses, churches, stores, mills, and other buildings, as well as former roads and forest paths, even some old cemeteries.

Townspeople, struck with shock and despair, began getting the alarming knocks on their doors by so-called men in black in 1916, and within a year, the monumental task of making way for the reservoir by clearing the landscape and dismantling towns—and lives—began.

DAMMING LIVES

When Providence was founded in 1936, residents relied on private wells—which, as the small yet burgeoning settlement that it was, proved adequate. But over the course of a century, its booming population meant that a central water supply was critical. In 1773, what's known as a "fountain society" was created; this provided water throughout the city through a network of hollowed out logs. (Some of these have since been unearthed during city public works projects.) Later, in the 1870s, as the metropolis continued to flourish, the lower Pawtuxet River in Cranston was developed to churn out further gallons.

But by the 1910s, the quality of Pawtuxet water became progressively poorer as the result of pollution from the Industrial Revolution, and its flow was expected to imminently fall short of rising demand. Providence was desperate for a new, central, reliable source to support its growing base of residents, businesses, and industry, as well as to help quelch fires.

In 1913, a water supply board was established to identify an area that could do just that; their initial meetings were purportedly held in secret. They soon zoned in on Scituate in the north-central part of the state. With the bountiful Ponaganset River, Moswansicut River, and the northern branch of the Pawtuxet River flowing through it, it was an ideal location for the much-needed reservoir. It was also uphill, relatively close to Providence, and water could flow to the capital gravity-fed.

But to support a substantial reservoir and dam would require a large area in a state of just 1,214 square miles—which would necessitate a sacrifice.

The board identified all or parts of Scituate's village towns of Rockland, Kent, Ashland, Wilbur Hollow, South Scituate, North Scituate, Richmond, Saundersville, Ponaganset, and Clayville for this condemnation. Some would be completely immersed in water; others would be cleared to establish the reservoir's watershed.

All this would require an exodus of roughly 1,600 rural folk—hard-working families of farmers and mill workers, many who had lived in their towns for generations.

THE FLOW OF HISTORY

Settled in 1700 and formally incorporated in 1731, Scituate, like many New England towns, was at first a thriving agricultural community. Because of the plentiful rivers and streams that flowed through it and around it, gristmills and sawmills soon went up, and with the 1800s came booming industrial growth. By 1900, four mills were in operation in Rockland, Clayville, Ponaganset, and Richmond; these manufactured, spun, and dyed shoe and corset laces. What's more, the Clayville mill even sold its excess electricity to outlying towns.

Owned and operated by William E. Joslin, these mills employed dozens of workers, the majority of them the soon-to-be displaced.

But this was hardly a concern for Providence. In 1915, a new Providence Water Supply Board was established, and on April 9 of that year, the state General Assembly approved their purchase of 23.1 square miles in Scituate under a relatively unfamiliar concept (in the residential sense, at least), of "eminent domain." Many locals and historians consider that day, when the "Pure Water for Providence" ordinance was passed, as "Black Friday."

The committee, which had been granted substantial powers by the city and state, immediately began securing contracts for the erection of a dam and aqueducts, and residents were soon notified of their fates by representatives of the water board soon referred to as "men in black."

Indubitably, public outcry and lawsuits followed, but the board surged forward in its doomful task, undeterred. By the time the communities heard about it, their fates had already been decided.

A century later, Shirley Arnold, a Scituate historian and ancestor to a forced-out family, described the turmoil and trauma. "People didn't really understand what was happening," she told one local researcher.

Ray Wolf, author of *The Lost Villages of Scituate*, has echoed that forlorn sentiment. "They just couldn't comprehend that someone they called 'The Man from Providence' could just show up one day and tell them they had to move," he lamented to the *Johnston Sunrise*.

As the work hastened, residents were compensated for their losses—for what many considered an unfair, pinny-pinching sum—and they began to abandon their homes and filter out of the doomed towns. Commercial buildings were auctioned off, at below-value prices, to whoever wanted the materials; trolley tracks were ripped up; power lines removed; and mill machinery pulled out and hauled away to other factories.

As Arnold has noted, her family was in Scituate long before the town was incorporated, and they never got over the grief and bitterness of being reluctantly uprooted. "You can imagine how they might have felt—over 200 years of family history, gone."

Some left underscoring their shock and grief with bold statements.

In May 1916, for instance, the Knight family received $12,150 for their holdings of 406 acres, two barns, and an icehouse; the sale also included two houses, "1 burned"—by the family as a sort of effigy.

Others refused to accept their dire fates.

There were several suicides: A farmer in Ponaganset told his family he was going out to feed the livestock; they later found that he had hanged himself in the barn. Another grieving resident slit his own throat.

Former Rockland resident and prolific poet Helen O. Larson wrote about that tragedy:

> *The city lawyer tried to buy one elderly man's home;*
> *He said I was born here and I'll die here;*
> *So, he cut his throat and died in his bedroom alone.*

Mill owner Joslin's family fought a long, ultimately losing legal battle; in protest, the millionaire constructed a fancy dance hall in Richmond in 1919, knowing that it would be razed.

In the end, though, Joslin worked out well in the bargain: He was granted $1.5 million for his holdings in the ill-fated towns. His prosperous Joslin Manufacturing Company—which owned and operated several mills in Scituate and Providence and once billed itself as the "largest and most complete shoelace manufactory in the world"—was broken up in 1925.

Still, his compensation was a hefty sum at the time, and in that regard, he was in the minority. Given paltry payoffs, most residents were simply forced out, left to find new homes and start new lives elsewhere.

A MOMENTOUS UNDERTAKING

To make way for the reservoir and dam required the removal and demolition of 1,195 buildings. These included 375 homes, 223 barns, seven schools, six churches, eleven icehouses, thirty dairy farms, as well as several mills, post offices, taverns, general stores, blacksmith and wheelwright shops and fire stations, not to mention the Providence and Danielson Electric Railway.

Then there were the cemeteries. There were thousands of bodies buried throughout the villages; workers were given the painstakingly morbid job of disinterring them by hand and dislodging their headstones and footstones. Some of the dead were entombed for a second time in surrounding areas, but most were reburied at a newly created cemetery at the left tip of the reservoir in Clayville.

Even by most cemetery standards, it is a morose and lonely resting place, hidden away on a hilly clearing. It's been said that they were reinterred in the exact rows and locations as they originally had been—only they could say for sure, as any of their immediate family members now join them in eternal rest. And some, whose markers were not moved along with them, are truly lost to time.

As are others: Several hundred are said to remain undisturbed from their everlasting slumber beneath the depths of the reservoir.

In a similar reverential gesture, prior to the start of work, the Providence Water Supply Board hired a photographer to capture structures and landscapes in soon-to-be-flooded areas, as well as the progression of the project and workers going about their grim duties.

One of these black and white images depicts a "man in black" in a long trench coat walking stoically along a set of train tracks; in the background are trees bereft of leaves, homes, and a small barn slightly askew, its wooden façade blackened by the elements. Others show fields churning with smoke as homes and trees were burned; workers clearing scrub and logs; still more leading horse carts hauling away debris. Many of these images have been collected in Wolf's *The Lost Villages of Scituate*.

The first phase of the $20 million project involved leveling the former village of Kent in 1917, a feat that required horse and mule teams, steam shovels, and hundreds of laborers. These roughly 450 workers lived in an area known as "Winston Camp" throughout the years'-long clearing project, which involved not only building-leveling and burning, but stripping topsoil to accommodate the land as a lakebed, felling thousands of trees, and replanting seven million others in the watershed area to act as filters against contamination.

Construction of the 3,200-foot Kent dam (now the Gainer Memorial Dam) began in the early 1920s and was completed in 1925. It took the 23.1-square-mile reservoir a year to fill; today it holds fifty-six billion gallons of water and has a depth of between thirty-two and eighty-seven feet.

The treatment plant began operation in September 1926, and as the reservoir's water began to flow by aqueduct to Providence, the city heralded it with an opening ceremony complete with a speech by Providence mayor Joseph H. Gainer (for whom the dam is now named). That steady stream continues to this day.

The clearing of towns and land, tree transplantation, dam construction and filling of the reservoir remains the largest public works project in the history of Rhode Island. And a century later, the reservoir is still the state's largest water supply.

REMEMBRANCES

But, too, many bittersweet memories and resentments of the price of that progress endure.

Arnold, for her part, collected oral histories from a half-dozen or so survivors, but she recalls that many of the heartbroken displaced—including her family members—couldn't even talk about that fissure in their lives some decades later.

One former resident who did prolifically document her memories and grief was Larson, as recalled by her son Wolf. A resident of Rockland, she was six when the dislocation started, and thirteen when her family relocated to nearby Hope (a seemingly fitting name for a new home).

A nonagenarian when she died, she penned more than 1,700 poems in her lifetime, many of them about her time in Rockland— both the good times and the struggles. She wrote her first on a blackboard at age twelve just as workers had begun tearing down the building; her last just days before her death.

The stanza of one, "The Scituate Reservoir" reads:

The land was condemned the people were told;
Everyone felt sorry for the folks who were old;
People in Providence needed clean water to drink;
The city bought five villages; people had to sign with pen and ink;
Some folks were born there, some lived there for years;
They just couldn't seem to shake off their tears.

Perhaps as a further blow to her sadness, her childhood home had sat on a small hill just above the watershed, so its former location is still visible. Wolf has recalled regular trips accompanying her to view the spot. This Larson wrote about as well:

I go back now and then, the foundations are still there;
I turn around and walk away, in my heart a silent prayer;
We all know the reservoir has been there many years;
And I still believe it was filled with the people's tears.

Perhaps, in the end, she was right.

Sources

I am truly indebted to the many historians, researchers, and authors who have dedicated themselves to chronicling the histories of abandoned and forgotten towns. Thank you for your diligence and passion. I can only hope to do you—and them—justice.

Books/Research Papers

Blanchard, Fessenden S., "Ghost Towns of New England: Their Ups and Downs," Dodd, Mead & Company, 1960.

Citro, Joseph A., *Weird New England: Your Travel Guide to New England's Local Legends and Best Kept Secrets*, Sterling Publishing Co., Inc., 2010.

D'Agostino, Thomas, *Abandoned Villages and Ghost Towns of New England*, Schiffer Publishing Ltd., 2008.

Howe, Lauren, "Past, Present, and Future: The Effects of the Death of the Swift River Valley and the Birth of the Quabbin Reservoir on Local Residents," 2009; https://www.academia.edu/1455602/Past _Present_and_Future_The_Effects_of_the_Death_of_the_Swift _River_Valley_and_the_Birth_of_the_Quabbin_Reservoir_on _Local_Residents.

Ignasher, Jim, *Remembering Smithfield: Sketches of Apple Valley*, The History Press, 2009.

Lord, Nina Way, *Ollie's Davidson*, Northeast Publishing Co., 1988.

Paradis, Summer, and McManus, Cathy, *Gone But Not Forgotten: New England's Ghost Towns, Cemeteries, and Memorials*, Schiffer Publishing Ltd., 2013.

Pedersen, Margo, "Malaga Island: How the State of Maine Devastated a Resilient Island Community in the Name of the Greater Good"; https://www.nhd.org/sites/default/files/PedersenSrPaper.pdf.

Plumb, Taryn, *Haunted Boston*, Globe Pequot Press, 2016.

Resch, Tyler, *Glastenbury: The History of a Vermont Ghost Town*, The History Press, 2008.

Richardson, Eleanor Motley, *Hurricane Island: The Town That Disappeared*. Island Institute in cooperation with Hurricane Island Outward Bound School, 1989.

Young, Hazel, "Islands of New England," Little, Brown and Company, 1954.

Newspaper/Web-based articles

American Ancestors by the New England Historic Genealogical Society, Vita Brevis, "Lost Towns of the Quabbin," September 4, 2019.

Bamberg, Jane M., "The Scituate Reservoir"; https://www.wpwa.org /documents/education/Bamberg.%20Scituate%20Reservoir.pdf.

Bangs, B.J., "The Legend of Boobytown: From Lewiston to Lower Dallas Plantation," *Discover Maine: Western Maine*, Volume 27, Issue 4, 2018.

Bashour, Mark J., and Levia, Delphis L., "Interpreting the Place Space of an Extinct Cultural Landscape: The Swift River Valley of Central Massachusetts," *Historical Journal of Massachusetts* Volume 34, No. 2, Summer 2006.

Bavoso, Katharine, "Maine Mysteries: The Drowned Ghost Town of Flagstaff," *News Center Maine*, July 27, 2016.

Bennett, Ashleigh, "Traces of Time," *Cape Cod Life*, August 2010.

Bushnell, Mark, "Then Again: The Rise and Fall of the Ely Copper Mines," *VTDigger.org*, October 21, 2018.

Capecod.com, "Hidden Cape Cod: A Village That Used to Exist in Provincetown," September 2, 2021; https://www.capecod.com /lifestyle/hidden-cape-cod-a-village-that-used-to-exist-in -provincetown.

Conkling, Philip, "Hurricane Island," *The Maine Mag*, November 2015.

SOURCES

Cook, Greg, "Plans Underway to Resurrect Waterbury's Holy Land USA," *Wonderland*, April 19, 2019.

Connecticut's Victorian Outdoor Museum, "Greetings from Johnsonville Village"; https://johnsonville.omeka.net.

Corriveau, David, "Cost of Ely Mine Cleanup Climbs to $24M, but Timetable for Start Uncertain," *Valley News*, August 28, 2019.

Dubrule, Deborah, "Malaga Revisited: On a Casco Bay Island, A Shameful Incident in Maine's History Comes to Light," *The Working Waterfront*, August 1, 2005.

Gagnon, Dawn, "Bangor Ghost Hunters Probe Site of Former Tannery Town," *Bangor Daily News*, October 30, 2009.

Gannaway, Wayne, "A Pilgrimage to Waterbury," *Connecticut Explored*, Summer 2008.

Harrington, Daniel F., "Opinion/Harrington: The Heartbreaking, Magnificent Birth of a Treasure," *The Providence Journal*, August 29, 2020.

Herwick III, Edgar B., "The Towns that Were Lost so that Boston Could Have Clean Water," *GBH News*, May 14, 2014.

Hillenbrand, Randall, "The Oneida Community"; http://www.nyhistory .com/central/oneida.htm.

I95, "The Abandoned Town of Johnsonville CT: Then and Now." https://i95rock.com/the-abandoned-ghost-town-of-johnsonville -ct-then-now.

Ignasher, Jim, "Where was Skeeterville?" *The Smithfield Times*, February 2015.

Johnston Sunrise, "Submerged But Not Forgotten: The Lost Villages of Scituate," September 16, 2009.

Kiernan, John, "What's in the Water in Scituate?" *Rhode Island Monthly*, May 2, 2017.

Klein, Maury, "The Scituate Reservoir: A Reminder of the Price of Progress," *41N Magazine*, November 20, 2015.

Kloczko, Justin, "Inside Johnsonville, the Victorian Ghost Town That No One in Connecticut Wants," *Vice*, September 22, 2015.

Lehman, Eric D., "The Legend of Pleasure Beach," Bridgeport Library, Bridgeport History Center (n.d.).

SOURCES

Long, Burke O., "The Children of Malaga Island," Bowdoin College (n.d.).

Maine Department of Fisheries and Wildlife, Wildlife Division, "A History and Self-Guiding Tour of Swan Island" (n.d.).

Maineboats.com, "The Other Swan Island: A Jewel on the Kennebec" (n.d.).

McKown, Colleen, and Robin, Josh, "Malaga Island: How to Rectify a Racist Past," *Spectrum News*, September 26, 2021.

——, "On Island Beauty, a Buried Story of How Maine Exiled a Thriving Fishing Village," *Spectrum News*, September 26, 2021.

——, "Retelling Malaga Island's Story through Art," *Spectrum News*, August 25, 2021.

Marteka, Peter, "A Nature Hike Tours a 19th-Century Iron-Making Complex at Roxbury's Mine Hill Preserve," *Connecticut Magazine*, September 29, 2020.

Milner, Surya, "The Legacy of Malaga Island and the Limits of Maine's Progressivism," *Catapult Magazine*, August 24, 2020.

Mitenbuler, Reid, "The Stubborn American Who Brought Ice to the World," *The Atlantic*, February 5, 2013.

Moorehead, Jacquelyn, "Local Man Shares Reservoir's Complicated Century-Long History," *Valley Breeze & Observer*, September 19, 2018.

Musante, Fred, "For Want of a Bridge, a Season's Undone," *The New York Times*, June 30, 1996.

Nemitz, Bill, "After 98 Years, An Apology Long Overdue," *Portland Press Herald*, September 17, 2010.

The New England Historical Society, "Jacataqua, the Indian Sachem Who Bore Aaron Burr's Love Child" (n.d.).

New Hampshire Public Radio, "Haverhill: 250 Years in the Making," October 25, 2013.

Ocker, J. W., "Livermore Is a Strange Name for a Ghost Town," *New Hampshire Magazine*, July 15, 2020.

Parker, Paul Edward, "R.I.'s Missing Ghost Town: What Happened to the People in Hanton City, and Where Did They Come From?" *Providence Journal*, November 3, 2019.

SOURCES

Perreault, Denise, "Lost Village of Rockland Remembered at History Conference," *Valley Breeze & Observer*, April 29, 2015.

Plumb, Taryn, "Come and Gone," *The Boston Globe*, December 10, 2009.

Rathsmill, Victoria, "Middlesex Fells: Haywardville Returns from the Past," *Wicked Local*, April 23, 2014.

Reitz, Stephanie, "For 4 Towns, Quabbin Is a Reservoir of Grief," *Associated Press*, April 27, 2008.

Rhode Island Historical Preservation Commission, "Historic and Architectural Resources of Scituate, Rhode Island: A Preliminary Report," May 1980.

———, "Historic and Architectural Resources of Smithfield, Rhode Island," May 1980.

Robinson, Melia, "A Connecticut Ghost Town that Nobody Wanted to Buy Finally Sold for $1.85 Million," *Business Insider*, July 11, 2017.

Rogers-Bull, Marilyn, "Solon & Beyond: The Day We Had to Abandon Our Homes in the Name of Progress," *The Town Line*, July 22, 2020.

———, "Solon & Beyond: More on the Burial of Flagstaff," *The Town Line*, July 29, 2020.

———, "Solon & Beyond: The Burial of Flagstaff Story Continues," *The Town Line*, August 5, 2020.

———, "Solon & Beyond: The Conclusion of the Burial of Flagstaff," *The Town Line*, August 12, 2020.

Rosenberg, Elisabeth C., "A Community of Necessity: The Quabbin Reservoir's History and the Future of 'Managed Retreat,'" *History News Network* (n.d.).

Roxbury Land Trust, "Mine Hill: A National Historic Landmark" (n.d.).

Sarnacki, Aislinn, "1-Minute Hike: Swan Island in the Kennebec River," *Bangor Daily News*, June 20, 2017.

Smith, Nicola, "Lost in Vershire, 'Ely War' Site Slowly Sinks into the Forest," *Valley News*, June 26, 2017.

Strange New England, "The Drowned Villages of Maine," June 22, 2020.

Sullivan, James, "Monson Was a Ghost Town Long before This Pandemic," *The Boston Globe*, April 9, 2020.

Tepfer, Daniel, "Pleasure Beach: What's Left Isn't Much Fun," *CT Post*, September 7, 2009.

Tuohy, Lynne, "In 1929, Enfield, Mass., Was Quite a Quiet Little Town. But Boston Was Thirsty. So in 1938, They Razed the Buildings, and Flooded the Land," *Hartford Courant*, December 13, 1999.

Vermonter.com, "Exploring Ricker Basin, a Vermont Ghost Town Long Abandoned" (n.d.).

Walsh, Kate, "Visit the Ruins of Waterbury's Little River Settlement," StoweToday.com, June 21, 2010.

Weekes, Julia Ann, "Settlers May Have Abandoned Monson Center in 1770, But It's a Pretty Ghost Town Today," *The New Hampshire Union Leader*, July 30, 2020.

Weizel, Richard, "Long Beach Road Work Gets Underway," *CT Post*, March 3, 2010.

Williams, Tate, "Washed Away," *The Magazine*, September 11, 2014.

Websites

Cow Hampshire blog, www.cowhampshireblog.com

Forest, Parks and Recreation Vermont, vtstateparks.com

Hill Historical Society, www.hillhistoricalsociety.com

Holy Land USA, www.holylandwaterbury.org

Hurricane Island Center for Science and Leadership, www.hurricaneisland.net

Ghost Towns, www.ghosttowns.com

Lighthouse Friends, www.lighthousefriends.com

Logging in Lincoln, logginginlincoln.com

Maine Coast Heritage Trust, www.mcht.org

The Maine Memory Network, www.mainememory.net

Monomoy National Wildlife Refuge, www.fws.gov/refuge/Monomoy

New England Lighthouses: A Virtual Guide, www.newenglandlighthouses.net

Old Pleasure Beach, http://oldpleasurebeachct.com

The Oneida Community Mansion House, www.oneidacommunity.org

Only In Your State, www.onlyinyourstate.com

The Rhode Island Historical Society, www.rihs.org

SOURCES

Roxbury Land Trust, Roxburylandtrust.org
Sandy River & Rangeley Lakes Railroad, www.srrl-rr.org
Society for the Protection of New Hampshire Forests, forestsociety.org
Town of Franconia website, www.franconianh.org
The Trustees of Reservations, thetrustees.org
U.S. Fish and Wildlife Service, www.fws.gov/refuge/Monomoy
WhiteMountainHistory.org, whitemountainhistory.org

About the Author

Taryn Plumb is a longtime journalist based in New England. She has authored *Shipwrecks and other Maritime Disasters of the Maine Coast*, *Haunted Boston*, *New England UFOs*, *Haunted Maine Lighthouses*, and the 10th edition of *Maine Off the Beaten Path*. She also continued Nancy Roberts' celebrated *Haunted Houses*.